The Graduate School Funding Handbook

Second Edition

The Graduate School Funding Handbook

April Vahle Hamel

with Mary Morris Heiberger
and Julia Miller Vick

SECOND EDITION

PENN

University of Pennsylvania Press

Philadelphia

Copyright © 1994, 2002 by April Vahle Hamel

All rights reserved

Printed in the United States of America on acid-free paper

10 9 8 7 6 5 4 3 2 1

Published by

University of Pennsylvania Press

Philadelphia, Pennsylvania 19104-4011

Library of Congress Cataloging-in-Publication Data

Hamel, April Vahle.

    The graduate school funding handbook / April Vahle Hamel with Mary Morris Heiberger and Julia Miller Vick.—2nd ed.

        p. cm.

    Includes bibliographical references and index.

    ISBN 0-8122-1810-8 (pbk. : alk. paper)

    1. Universities and colleges—United States—Graduate work—Finance.

2. Graduate students—Scholarships, fellowships, etc.—United States. I. Heiberger, Mary Morris. II. Vick, Julia Miller. III. Title.

LB2371.4 .H35 2002

378.3′3′0973—dc21

                                              2001057463

Contents

Preface to the Second Edition

This second edition of *The Graduate School Funding Handbook* contains new and updated information. Chapter 1, for example, has been expanded to include data about distance learning. All of the grants, fellowships, and scholarships offered by the government and private foundations have been thoroughly researched, revised, and brought up to date. Some funding opportunities listed in the first edition have been removed because they are no longer offered, while others have been combined and rewritten, as with the Department of Defense Science and Engineering Fellowships. Information on new awards such as the Paul and Daisy Soros Fellowships for New Americans has been added.

Chapter 1
Graduate Degrees, Institutional Financial Aid, and Graduate School Application Tips

The purpose of this book is to cast light on the murky world of graduate school funding. Of special focus are master's and doctoral programs in the arts and sciences and in engineering. Conversations with undergraduates as well as other potential graduate school applicants make it clear that institutions offer piecemeal information, at best, about institutional as well as external funding. Even with daily improvements of university and funding agency web sites, it is often difficult to locate good, comprehensive financial aid data.

In this chapter we will first look at the bare essentials of graduate education: graduate degree types; the nature of institutional financial aid; external financial aid; the affordability of graduate school; and tips on applying to graduate school. Subsequent chapters will examine specific external funding opportunities and grant and fellowship proposal-writing strategies in greater detail.

Types of Graduate Degrees

In 2001, more than 2.1 million students were enrolled in graduate programs around the United States. In any given year, graduate schools across the country award nearly 500,000 graduate degrees. Given the enormous number of students enrolled in advanced degree programs, it is important to define the categories and degree options. We have classified graduate programs into the general categories described in the rest of this section. Table 1 provides a summary of this information.

Master's Degree Programs

Applied or professional master's programs require one to three years of course work and are constructed to prepare people for careers in the

TABLE 1. Types of Degree Programs and Sampling of Degrees Offered

Master's

Applied/professional	M.A.B.M.	Master of Agribusiness Management
	M.Adm.J.	Master of Administration of Justice
	M.A.M.B.	Master of Applied Molecular Biology
	M.A.P.	Master of Applied Psychology
	M.Arch.	Master of Architecture
	M.B.A.	Master of Business Administration
	M.S.W.	Master of Social Work
Research	M.A.	Master of Arts
	M.S.	Master of Science
Creative	M.F.A.	Master of Fine Arts
	M.F.A.W.	Master of Fine Arts in Writing
	M.M.	Master of Music

Doctoral

Applied/professional	D.B.A.	Doctor of Business Administration
	D.C.	Doctor of Chiropractic
	D.Ed. or Ed.D.	Doctor of Education
	D.D.S.	Doctor of Dental Surgery
	D.Sc.A.	Doctor of Applied Science
	D.V.M.	Doctor of Veterinary Medicine
Research	D.Sc. or Sc.D.	Doctor of Science
	D.Th.	Doctor of Theology
	Ph.D.	Doctor of Philosophy

professions. Master's degrees in business administration (M.B.A.), teaching (M.A.T.), social work (M.S.W.), and others fall into this category.

Many of these degree programs include some sort of internship or hands-on experience. Social work schools, for example, usually require a practicum as part of the curriculum.

Experience in the field between undergraduate and graduate school matriculation is often highly desirable. Business schools generally prefer applicants who have had some business-related work experience to those who have not. Older students are often found in these programs.

Research master's programs require one to two years of course work and are designed to enhance research experience begun in undergraduate school by bringing previously learned investigative skills to a more sophisticated level.

For completion of the degree requirement, some programs require a long research paper called a thesis. In addition, most expect successful performance in written and/or oral examinations and possibly a series of papers. Most research master's programs (M.A., M.S.) in the arts and sciences (English, history, biology, economics, etc.) fall into this category.

Many students in these programs wish to extend their knowledge in a field in order to prepare for doctoral work or to improve their job prospects. A student interested in foreign service might get a master's in international studies, for instance. Still others enroll for the sake of deepening their knowledge base.

Creative master's programs last two to three years and are intended to expand on creative work started in undergraduate school or through other experience.

Painters, photographers, musicians, poets, and artists of all sorts are attracted to creative programs in fine arts (M.F.A.), music (M.M.), writing and poetry (M.F.A.W.), and others.

Creative programs usually include a project such as a book of poetry, a recital, or an exhibition as part of the curriculum.

While students in these fields may have various career aims, all usually intend to continue their creative work. Graduates in these fields often acquire teaching certification for elementary or secondary education or pursue a research doctorate in a related field. An individual with an M.F.A. in printmaking might get secondary education certification in order to teach at the high school level.

Doctoral Programs

Applied/professional doctoral programs such as those found in business (D.B.A.), medicine (M.D.), law (J.D.), and education (Ed.D.), like their applied and professional master's counterparts, are designed to develop a corps of new professionals who will apply their skills in a hands-on style. Graduates with these degrees may stay on to teach or do research in college or university settings, but most aim at careers outside of higher education. A physician, for example, may practice in a single, group, or institutional practice, do full-time clinical teaching or research at a medical school, or combine clinical practice and teaching, but most M.D.s will spend their careers in private or institutional clinical practice.

The length of study in these programs ranges from three to four years of full-time enrollment. The applied doctorate may additionally require postdoctoral experience and/or passing of national licensing examinations as a prerequisite for active participation in the profession. Both law and medicine have postgraduate examinations—on a national level for medicine and on a state level for law.

The *research doctorate* almost always culminates in the awarding of the Ph.D. or Sc.D. degree. Although the degree stands for "doctor of philosophy" it is qualified by the addition of the field of study, as in "doctor of philosophy in French literature." Most research doctoral degree programs are found in arts and sciences or engineering, but are also available in business, social work, and other professional areas. Students in these programs usually intend to do research in higher education, industry, or government, or they plan to teach at the college or university level. In many instances a combination of research and teaching is the predictable career goal.

The length of time needed to complete a research doctorate ranges from four to eight years, depending on the discipline. Students spend two to three years in course work, one to three years doing research in a field within the discipline (like nineteenth-century intellectual history within history), and then one to three years writing a major research paper called a dissertation. A dissertation can range in length from 100 to 700 pages.

Students in science usually finish more quickly than those in humanities. Social science time to degree completion varies by discipline and can be shorter for economists but longer for anthropologists, who must engage in lengthy research, often abroad. In general, Ph.D. dissertation completion speed is determined by the focus and organization of the program, the requirements of the field, and the determination of the individual student. Students often bog down at the dissertation writing stage, dragging degree completing out for years.

It is not usually necessary to obtain a master's degree before entering a research doctoral program. One can apply directly to a Ph.D. or other type of doctoral program with a bachelor's degree. In some doctoral programs students are enrolled first in the master's program and then automatically moved to the doctoral level a year later. In some programs a master's degree is awarded automatically after thirty hours of course work, although many programs require examinations of some sort. As a rule, it is better to apply to a doctoral program immediately because the chances of receiving a fellowship are much better.

At points in each program, doctoral students take a series of written and oral examinations. Sometimes these tests are called qualifying examinations and must be passed within the first two years of the program in order to continue in the program. This practice is common, for example, in economics. In other programs, comprehensive examinations are taken after the completion of course work. Success in these examinations is required before preparation of the dissertation proposal.

Although time to degree is shorter on average in the sciences, those graduates usually enter postdoctoral training programs after they have received their degrees. This transitional time between degree completion and entry into the profession can vary according to program and job availability. The length of these "postdocs," as they are called, can be from one to five years. While postdocs are not as common in the social sciences and humanities, they are becoming more prevalent as time goes on. See Chapter 7 for more information on this subject.

Combined Degree Programs

Combining applied and research degree programs is not unusual. A master's student in social work may also pursue a law degree; an M.D. matriculant may be a concurrent student in a Ph.D. biology program. If you are interested in combining programs, be sure to ask how it works at the places to which you are applying. Ordinarily, applications are submitted to both programs, and the applicant must be accepted in both. Occasionally an established combined program may require only a single application.

Certificate Programs

It is not uncommon for universities to offer certificates that will satisfy state or other agency requirements. In some cases, the certificate may be related to licensing requirements within the field. People in education may need a number of certifications in order to work as teachers, counselors, or administrators.

Other certificates may not lead to licensing or a degree but may be a university's way of recognizing the acquisition of skills or information in a particular area. For example, certification in women's studies may mean that a doctoral student in French literature has satisfied the university's requirements within an area of concentration. The certificate is viewed as an enhancement to the degree program.

University Financial Aid

General Information

Financial aid available to graduate students from or through universities comes in many forms. The types of funding for students in graduate school can differ drastically from what undergraduates are offered. Money offered to graduate students is allocated based on merit, need, or a combination of the two.

Professional schools tend to make need the primary barometer for awarding financial support. This means that the applicant does not own property over a certain value or have an income over a specified amount and is living in a relative state of poverty. Scholarships based on merit in professional schools are generally offered only to the top few applicants.

One notable exception occurs when administrators are trying to improve the program's rating. It is not unusual for a school or program to offer a large chunk of scholarship money to many of the very best prospects regardless of need. Through this financial inducement, applicants who might have gone to a higher ranked school are encouraged to attend a lower ranked program. A program with better students can attract better students. You should look for these opportunities, then balance the financial benefits, educational soundness, and career placement record of one school with another.

Arts and sciences master's and doctoral programs generally award scholarships and fellowships based primarily on merit. Applicants are ranked against one another for admissions based on their past scholarly performance and on their future academic potential. Financial need is not the primary factor.

In some instances, applicants offered merit fellowships must also pass a needs test. The U.S. Department of Education gives block training grants to selected departments, mostly in the sciences at numerous universities. The department requires student recipients to pass a needs test even though students may be selected first based on merit.

It is not unusual for university's various departments or schools to have more than one set of funding criteria. Business schools fund most M.B.A. students on a need-based system while most Ph.D. students are funded on a merit-based or merit-need based arrangement.

Three considerations drive student funding systems: first, how the program itself (including faculty and building costs) is financed; second, how many years students remain in the program; third, what kind of career earning potential graduates have.

Professional schools are financed primarily by undergraduate and graduate student tuition. Faculty salaries, career counselors, and staff are all paid mainly through tuition payments. This is the same principle that drives most undergraduate programs. Students are in professional programs two to four years, and most have substantial earning potential. These students can afford to pay their way based on potential earnings so most financial aid comes in the form of loans.

Arts and sciences funding considerations vary from those of professional schools. Undergraduates' tuition is used to fund graduate as well as undergraduate programs. This is especially true when graduate students are given stipends to work as teaching assistants in undergraduate classes.

There are universities where graduate tuition is an important component of financing programs and where students are expected to pay for their education, but this condition tends to be found in non-doctoral degree-granting institutions where the master's programs are more applied than research-oriented.

Other exceptions to the arts and sciences rule are the most competitive and prestigious doctorate-granting institutions which may admit people who want to be doctoral students at the master's level and charge them tuition and offer no fellowship money for at least the first year.

Most research doctoral students are not expected to support themselves through the initial stages of graduate school for several reasons. Their programs are too long, they perform important services in educating undergraduates and helping facilitate faculty research, and they have limited postgraduate earning potential. Attorneys may earn up to $100,000 a year their first year out of law school, whereas an English Ph.D. is lucky first to get a full-time job and then may earn $38,000 a year. The lawyer spent three years in graduate school, but the English Ph.D. may have been there seven or eight.

To recruit students into long programs with limited earning potential, universities must offer some form of solid financial, no-payback support to the most qualified students.

Private and public universities often approach doctoral student financial aid differently, offering a variety of combinations of no-work fellowships, teaching or research (work required) assistantships, and loans. Owing to their lower tuition rates, state schools may not be able to provide money to students for as many years as private institutions. First-year graduate students may be expected to work as teaching assistants in a public university but not always at a private counterpart, where first-year fellowships may allow students to concentrate completely on course work.

Programs within the same university will have different sorts of financial support packages for their applicants. These may include tuition waivers, fellowships, assistantships, work-study jobs and loans. It is important to know what kind of support is available, how long the support can be expected to last, and the amount of funding available. No prospective graduate student should go blindly into a program without knowing the short- and long-term financial consequences. And any doctoral student who is not offered a fellowship or a teaching or research assistantship by the second year should look at other institutions or other career paths.

A summary of types of funding that universities may offer to applicants and continuing students follows.

Tuition Waivers

Tuition waivers (tuition remission or tuition scholarships) reduce the amount of tuition a student has to pay. Sometimes tuition waivers cover the whole tuition bill while others pay part of the cost. No money changes hands and the award is not considered taxable income, and students are not expected to pay it back. Students may receive non-negotiable tuition vouchers which are presented at registration. When applying to all types of master's and doctoral programs, you should inquire about the availability of tuition waivers and whether they are awarded on a need or merit basis. In arts and sciences, most doctoral and many master's students receive these scholarships.

Fellowships

Fellowships are actual dollars paid in addition to tuition waivers. Fellowships are support for room, board, and supplies and are taxable as income. The money is generally referred to as a stipend. There is no payback expected and students are not required to work for these funds. Fellowships are usually offered by universities for the first year of study and for the dissertation writing year for doctoral students. They are given to master's and doctoral students in all types of programs but are found most often in doctoral programs in research fields.

Fellowships almost always come from the university the student is attending but sometimes a student may apply to an outside agency such as the National Science Foundation (NSF) for a portable fellowship, which may be taken to any graduate institution.

Assistantships

Assistantships require some performance of duties in exchange for a stipend. The stipend is usually larger than would ordinarily be paid for the type of work done. Students who function as teaching assistants generally get paid more for their work than part-time instructors do.

There are three forms of assistantships: teaching, research, and graduate assistantships. They are found in the greatest numbers in engineering and arts and sciences programs, but other programs also offer assistantships. In the biomedical sciences, research assistantships are much more important than teaching assistantships. Depending on the type of institution and the programs they offer, both master's and doctoral students may be eligible for these stipends.

Teaching Assistantships

A teaching assistantship requires five to twenty hours a week of assisting a professor with classes, or, independently teaching a course. The former is more common than the latter. Teaching assistants (TAs) supervise laboratory sections, run discussion groups, assign and grade assignments, proctor and grade examinations, drill language students, help with equipment, tutor undergraduates, hold office hours, and lecture in class. In most large state and some private universities, TAs are responsible for handling a great deal of the instructional load. This is especially true in large institutions with serious financial constraints. The use of great numbers of teaching assistants has come in for intense criticism in recent times and TAs often feel overworked and exploited.

How Much Time Is Spent Being a TA?

Applicants are curious about how much time is devoted to being a TA and how that time might affect success in course work. The answer is not simple and can vary from department to department and from school to school. Some departments view the TA experience as fleeting, perhaps a semester or a year and requiring only five to seven hours a week. While TAs are found in most disciplines, they are more prevalent in arts and sciences, particularly in English and the foreign languages and laboratory sciences such as chemistry. In the social sciences and humanities, the hours a student devotes to being a TA are generally higher, sometimes up to twenty hours a week. In these areas undergraduate teaching needs are greatest. TAs in English composition courses often complain about the amount of time spent in teaching. Many feel the time to degree completion is lengthened because of unreasonable teaching expectations.

TAs: Employees, Union Members, or Students?

In some state and private universities, TAs are considered employees first and students second and may be unionized. In other institutions, teaching experience is considered an important part of the curriculum, and the duties of teaching assistants are conceptualized as academic rather than employment activities. The perspective a school takes has a great deal to do with how many hours TAs work and to which benefits they are entitled.

When TAs see themselves as overworked, underpaid lackeys without benefits, they may unionize, strike, or demonstrate for improved working conditions, better training, benefits, and respect. It is important to know how teaching assistants are viewed by the institutions and departments to which you are applying. Every prospective student should check to see whether there is serious TA unrest before accepting an offer of admission. These issues become very distracting and can poison an atmosphere that should encourage collegiality. You may decide to attend a university in the throes of conflict, but you should not do it unwittingly.

TA Training

In the not-so-distant past, TAs were untrained and at the mercy of their faculty leaders for direction about how to function successfully in the classroom or laboratory. Happily, serious TA training programs have been adopted at most reputable universities. Syracuse University has led the way in establishing rigorous training programs meant to help TAs feel comfortable and effective in their tasks. Training programs can include pre-registration workshops, ongoing seminars, videotaped practice lecturing, handbooks, and much more. Departments have also constructed programs to improve TA capabilities. This is another important area to investigate when applying to graduate programs.

Does Being a TA Really Lengthen the Time to Degree Completion?

The literature suggests that being a TA does not necessarily increase the time it takes to acquire a degree. Many observers believe that the TA experience is a beneficial intellectual segment that adds important socialization and skill-building components to graduate student life. Students who function as TAs can feel more integrated into their departments as well as into the rest of the academic life of the institution than those who do not have a TA role to fill. Most TAs function as junior faculty and are respected as such by undergraduates and faculty alike. In addition, a well-trained TA is a better future professor.

However, where TAs are overworked, bullied, and disrespected, the time to degree can be longer. If a student has unrelenting teaching duties that go on year after year and take up many hours a week, several things can happen. First, it becomes hard to balance study and research obligations with overwhelming teaching responsibilities. Next, the student may become discouraged and put off work toward degree completion. Then, students get angry at the department or the administration and become distracted from the goal of degree completion.

The ideal situation for a doctoral student is a work-free fellowship the first year, a teaching or research assistantship the next two years, and a work-free dissertation fellowship for degree completion.

Research Assistantships

Research assistantships are found primarily in departments where faculty members have large research grants that include support for students, postdocs, and research associates. Research assistants may also be found in areas where large training grants from the federal government are in place. These areas are usually in the sciences and engineering, and the sources for research and training grant funding include the National Institutes of Health, the National Science Foundation, the Department of Education, and the Department of Defense. Research assistants are engaged primarily, but not exclusively, in laboratory research. Generally, this research is seen as part of the curriculum. Students in these disciplines usually select a field within their discipline fairly quickly so that they can be placed in the appropriate lab. In some programs, students serve in a series of lab rotations and eventually select their area of specialization.

Since graduation rates in most of the sciences are fairly short compared to humanities, time to degree is not lengthened by research assistantships. In most cases the assistantship affords the student time to focus on their own research thus facilitating rather then impeding the march to graduation.

Graduate Assistantships

Another form of assistantship is referred to by the catch-all term graduate assistantship. Universities use graduate assistants for all sorts of tasks that do not fit into the teaching or research assistant category. Graduate assistants may spend time advising other students on topics ranging from finding part-time jobs to writing brochures. Graduate assistants may work in the graduate school compiling admission statistics, collating and assessing external funding information, or writing newsletters. In the best of all worlds, a GA works in an area that enhances his or her academic activities. An education student, for example, might advise teaching assistants or a psychology student might assist in the student counseling center.

College Work-Study

The federal government's College Work-Study Program has funding available through the Graduate and Professional Divisions. Although some of the monies from these programs go to support research and teaching assistants, a percentage is usually available to employ students in offices on campus.

Work-study employment is not necessarily related to a student's academic interest or the curriculum. The university is required to contribute to the student's pay; thus the government and the university share the cost of employing students while they are enrolled in course work. Most universities have federal work-study funds available for students at the graduate level. Work-study money is often given to departments that then find students to fill positions. For example, work-study students may work in a graduate school office doing reception work or in a departmental office doing clerical work.

Applicants who are not offered fellowships or teaching or research assistantships should always inquire about work-study opportunities. All students must establish financial need through a standard form available in the graduate school, department, or financial aid office. To be eligible for work-study, applicants must be U.S. citizens or permanent residents.

Loans

Loans are more readily available to U.S. citizens or permanent residents than to others. Money is borrowed under various federal government programs. Getting a loan, like getting college work-study, requires completing forms. These are found in the graduate school or financial aid office on all campuses. While most loans must be paid back with money, some programs have a *loan forgiveness program*. This means that work in a not-for-profit field for certain number of years after graduation may qualify graduates for forgiveness of part or all of the loans. If, for example, a law graduate works as a public defender or in a legal aid office for a specified number of years, the university may remove all or part of the loan indebtedness established during law school. The objective is to encourage career paths in low-paying but socially worthy professions.

Students should consider their postgraduate earning potential in deciding how much loan indebtedness can be realistically incurred.

External Grants and Fellowships

External funding comes from outside the university and is awarded directly to the student. Monies come from private foundations or agencies of the federal government. Sometimes the funds are paid to the student through the university, in other instances they are paid directly to the student.

Applicants should determine whether there is external money available in their area of study. The National Science Foundation (NSF), for example, offers 900 three-year fellowships for study in engineering, the sciences, and social sciences. This fellowship pays the student's tuition plus a cost of living stipend of $20,500 a year. Students in their last year of college or first year of graduate school are eligible to apply.

External fellowships also exist to encourage *underrepresented groups* to enroll in graduate programs, especially in the sciences and engineering. Members of minority groups and women should be alert to these opportunities.

In some cases money is available through the employer of an applicant's parent. Some universities have tuition benefit plans for children of faculty and staff. The money is usually for undergraduate tuition, but some schools do support graduate education for staff family members.

Certain ethnic organizations offer funding for graduate education. In addition, not-for-profit organizations such as the Epilepsy Foundation will support graduate student research.

Most of the rest of this book will examine external opportunities.

Should You Go to Graduate School?

Is graduate school right for you? Is it affordable? Will it facilitate your career goals? These are key questions every prospective graduate student should ask. There are no simple answers, but there are ways to determine whether going on in an educational setting makes sense. In a way, there is no separating intellectual from financial considerations, but motivation to learn, ambition to be in a certain career track, and enthusiasm to continue within or return to a classroom environment are the first topics with which you should deal.

If you are thinking of going to graduate school, do a thorough self-evaluation. Ask yourself the following questions:

1. Why do I want to continue my formal education?
2. What do I hope, in a very concrete way, to accomplish by acquiring an advanced degree?
3. Am I focused enough on my career track to start graduate school?
4. If I am in undergraduate school, should I take time off to get other kinds of experience, get more focused on my future, pay off undergraduate school debt, or travel around and see the world before committing to the rigors of graduate school?
5. Am I thinking of graduate school because that is what my parents want, because I can't get a job, because I am worried about paying off undergraduate loans, or because I can't think of anything better to do?
6. If I am already working, do I really need a graduate degree to enhance my career opportunities?
7. Can I attend a graduate program full-time or part-time?
8. If I am working, will my company share the tuition costs?
9. Will the investment of time and money needed to complete a graduate degree really pay off in the future?

Part of the investigation should include talking to recent graduates about whether their degree programs led to the career options they envisioned and whether the jobs they are doing are what you want to do. If you see yourself, for example, as a therapist, talk to several people in the field to see if you like what you hear about the job and what sort of graduate programs they chose. Ask what a typical day is like. Ask if they would have selected another path to their job. Therapists can get a degree in social work, psychology, or educational counseling. All these could lead to careers in counseling.

Sometimes another experience might be better than a graduate degree. Maybe an internship at the State Department is just as good or better than a graduate degree in international studies for securing a position in the foreign service.

Almost without exception a graduate degree should lead to or enhance a career. In a sense, all graduate programs are professional programs in that they should make employment possible or more satisfying or more financially rewarding.

Students who enter professional or applied programs are already aware of the career that should follow the degree, but students who enter master's programs in the arts and sciences are not always as directed toward work goals and are often disappointed at the end of the graduate experience. Too often graduate school is a safe extension of an education experience that began in kindergarten. It can be comforting to continue in the same pattern that has dominated a lifetime but it may be ill advised. Students who are clear about what graduate school can and will mean down the road make better choices about entering advanced degree programs.

Once a positive, well-informed decision has been made to move forward to the application process, then cost can be considered. Here are several questions to consider:

1. How much debt have I accumulated from undergraduate school? Would it be prudent to work for a while to reduce that load or would I be risking my advancement in the field by taking time off?
2. How long is it going to take me to get a degree and what is it going to cost? What will the university contribute in the way of tuition waivers, fellowships, or assistantships? How much money will I need to borrow?
3. Can my costs be reduced by going to a state institution?
4. Can I work for a company that will help pay my way through school?
5. Will the government pick up the costs for a work trade-off like going into the military or the Public Health Service?
6. Can I make enough money after graduation to pay off a significant

number of loans? Is a loan forgiveness program for public sector work available through my university?

7. Will family help with financial support?
8. Can I win external fellowships?
9. Can I work full-time or part-time and go to school?

Finding the answers to these questions is time-consuming but extraordinarily worthwhile.

In the end, the decision to go or not go to graduate school is very personal. There is no right answer; there is only your answer.

Selecting and Applying to Graduate School

There are four primary resources you can tap to find graduate programs best suited to your interest. These resources include: the Internet; publications; campus sources; and people who work in the field.

The Internet is a good place to start. Most universities now have sophisticated web sites that list all the graduate programs they offer. In addition, most departments have sites which detail the fields of study and degrees available. What you do not get from web sites, however, is how highly regarded the department is compared to others.

It is important to remember that the specific program quality is the most important factor when selecting a graduate school, not the overall ranking of the university. Not every program at a top-rated university is the very best. Sometimes a second-tier school has professional schools or departments that are rated the best.

One way to find out how a program is rated is through one of many *publications* such as *U.S. News and World Report* and *The Gourman Report,* which give rankings of various departments within universities.

Better sources of information are *faculty and other advising staff members* who are located on campus. Faculty in the field you want to enter can be especially insightful about which programs will best fit your interests. Faculty keep in close touch with their peers at other universities at annual meetings. The also read journal articles in their specialty areas which indicate where the latest research is being done. They should be able to give you contacts at other programs.

Many undergraduate schools have pre-professional advisors, especially in pre-med and pre-law. In pre-med it is especially important that you seek their advice and listen to what they have to say. In some schools the pre-med advisor is directly connected to the campus medical school and may sit in on admission decisions. This was true in my son's case. The pre-med advisor was influential in his admission to the medical school he attended.

Other campus advisors to tap may be located in the *career center*. Career center libraries usually have many books and pamphlets that describe and rate graduate programs. People who work in the field in which you have an interest can be very informative about what graduate school is like and what their experiences were. Young people, especially, have the most current information. Talking with a field professional has a lot of advantages. You can get a sense of what it is like to work in the profession, how successful a graduate program was in preparation for a career path, and what schools offer programs which might fit your interests.

Graduate Programs as Information Sources

Once you get a list of ten or so programs together, contact the departments or professional schools for detailed information packets.

If you are interested in an M.A. in English, contact the department, not the graduate school. Most graduate schools of arts and sciences are umbrella administrations that facilitate the admission and matriculation of students in numerous departments. They are good resources about whom to contact in departments and graduate student life in general, but not as informative as the departmental graduate advisor will be about program specifics.

Professional schools have their own admission advisors who can provide information packets as well as faculty who will be willing to answer questions about the program.

Knowing whom to talk to is only part of the research process. Finding out whether a program is right for you is crucial. Here are some questions you should ask of every program you are seriously considering:

1. Does the program have everything you need in the curriculum? Does is have the courses you need? Will the key faculty be around to teach them? More than one student has gone to a program only to find that the only faculty member with expertise in the field is on a two-year leave of absence.
2. Do you fit the admissions criteria with regard to academic background, grade-point average, and test scores? How many applicants are there each year and how many are accepted? Sometimes graduate guides like *Peterson's* will provide all of this information, especially for professional programs. For arts and sciences programs you may have to call or email to get this information.

You really do not want to waste time and money applying to a program to which you have absolutely no chance of being admitted.

To How Many Schools Should You Apply?

Under normal circumstances the rule is similar to that for undergraduate school. Apply to six to eight programs, some reaches, some probables, some back-ups. You may want to add an extra school in one or more categories, but don't waste too much time and money unless it is a common application to programs with small admissions percents like medical school.

Students in the upper 10 percent of the applicant pool have to be particularly careful not to apply to just the top six or so programs. When the rejection rate is 95 percent, as it can be in some small, highly prestigious programs, even the most qualified can be rejected by everyone. Students in the lower tier of the application pool may have to apply to more schools than most to maximize their options.

Be aware of state school preferences for state residents. Many of these universities must take a high percentage of in-state applicants. Be aware also of the home-court advantage that is sometimes the case when applying to a program at your undergraduate school. Some schools know their undergraduates are well trained and are enthusiastic to enroll them in their graduate programs. The University of Chicago and Harvard University are two institutions that love their own not only for graduate school admissions but for postgraduate employment as well.

Distance Learning or Traditional Graduate Schools?

More and more institutions now offer advanced degrees over the Internet. The student rarely, if ever, visits the campus and does all communication through the computer and the mail. These programs are more interactive than the old staple "correspondence learning," which is done completely through the mail. Some distance programs require some residency on campus, but many do not.

Many arguments rage about how good an education can be gotten by this method, but there is no doubt it is a mode of learning that is increasing rapidly in popularity. The lack of face-to-face interaction between student and faculty and student and student is often cited as educationally limiting. With advanced technology, however, interaction is increasing and Internet interaction and email can provide a dialog between teacher and student. Eventually video cameras will make contact more intimate.

For people with limited time and mobility, distance learning should be investigated. Beware, however, it is usually not any less expensive than traditional on-campus degree programs and, in some cases, is more costly. For people with the time to attend a traditional graduate program, the benefits of collegiality, classroom participation, and direct faculty contacts are many. Some predict we will abandon the classroom completely, but I would wager it will not be in the near future.

There are lots of publications out about distance learning which describe and rate the burgeoning programs throughout the country and the world. See the resource section at the end of this chapter.

Standardized Tests

Despite the continuing war against standardized tests, they are not going to be abandoned by graduate education in the near future. Most programs require some sort of general or area-specific test as a criterion for admission.

Many tests are no longer the paper-and-pencil version but a computer examination. The current computerized GRE, for example, gives an initial question or problem. A right answer generates a harder question; a wrong answer generates an easier question. The computer adjusts your score accordingly. You cannot skip a question. The Princeton Review advises that you must be especially careful at the beginning of each section and be very thoughtful when answering each question because there is no going back. Most students are now familiar enough with computers so that this format does not present a problem. Older students returning to academia need to practice their computer test-taking skills to become accustomed to this form of testing.

There is great argument about whether prepping helps improve scores. My own experience says yes, prepping can help. Improvement may not be dramatic, but can be substantive. What is the best way to go about it? Certainly buying a prep book and taking a sample test is a good start. And this should be done early, so that if a prep class is needed, time is available.

For GRE preparation, Princeton Review suggests that you buy Educational Testing's GRE POWERPREP for the most realistic practice of computer adaptive testing drills. Princeton Review carries a line of books for test prepping and has online practice testing sites. After taking a sample test and identifying any weaknesses, taking a course may be in order. A course may not be as helpful as it was during the pencil-and-paper days when the test involved a room full of people who answered a prescribed number of questions. No one should enter a test session, whether in a group or at an individual computer, completely cold. That would be foolish.

Standardized tests are important no matter what degree you are pursuing. They are a piece of the admission puzzle. Arguments are endless about how much emphasis, if any, should be put on these tests, but dependence on them will not change in the near future. When programs have large numbers of applicants for a small number of admissions, they will weed out with test scores and GPAs. Where admission percentages are high, standardized tests are not so important. In some areas, such as creative master's degree programs, samples of the creative process are much more important than test scores. Other departments may be more concerned with one part of a multiscored test than another. Language and literature departments are more concerned about GRE verbal scores than they are about the math results.

Be sure to find out how important standardized tests are to your program. That is easy for professional programs—they usually matter a great deal—but not so easy for others. Contact the department or school and ask first how important tests weigh on admission decisions and then what the average admit scores are for these exams.

References

All graduate schools ask for references. You want recommendations from those who know you as someone who will do well in an educational setting and who will write positively about your academic skills. Most graduate schools are not interested in character references. The best recommenders are those people who have had first-hand experience with your academic and professional potential and who can attest to those abilities. For arts and sciences programs, a senior faculty member who taught two or more of your courses is ideal. For professional graduate degree programs like an M.B.A., pick people who can testify to the quality of work you have done on the job or in an internship. Do not use teaching assistants or adjunct or part-time faculty (unless they are famous, and even then maybe not). While it may be unfair to rule them out, their opinions do not carry much weight because of their low status.

To help recommenders write the best possible letter consider doing the following.

1. Write a one-page synopsis about why you want to go to graduate school, what type of degree you want, and what your career goals are.
2. Provide the recommender with a transcript of your courses and grades and indicate in which courses, if any, he or she taught you.
3. Provide the recommender with copies of papers you have written for his or her course. If you are getting a work reference, provide reports you have written or summaries of projects you have undertaken. These give the recommender something concrete to refer to and something specific to write about.

The worst sort of reference letter in that in which nothing substantive is said. This can happen when the recommender does not know you well enough or cannot remember your work.

Some applicants take time off before they apply. In that case it is best to establish a credential file at your undergraduate school. Be sure the letters are current and reflect your graduate school interests. If you take several years between undergraduate and graduate school, keep in touch with your references. Drop them a postcard now and then, or call or drop in. College faculty should be important to you your whole life. Serious students need to bond with a faculty member, or a business mentor. If you have not established such a contact, do it now. Failure to have three enthusiastic recommenders who can speak to your potential is a grave mistake.

Filling out the Application

The application offers the opportunity to explain why you wish to enter a particular program, what it is about the field that attracts you, and the sort of career goals you have established. All components of the application are important. That includes grades, test scores, autobiographical data, and the essay. If your grades and test scores are so-so, the essay becomes crucial. An essay should demonstrate enthusiasm for the field, motivation to complete the program, an understanding of career goals. Everything should be enhanced by specific information, the more focused and detailed the better. Undergraduate applications often require cleverness and a range of diverse interests. Graduate applications require the communication of seriousness of purpose, maturity of intellectual thought, and complete focus on the field of study.

Deadlines

Earlier is better, especially with rolling admissions. Programs with deadlines always get a flurry of activity as the deadline approaches, which is an opportunity for communications to get misplaced. Be sure to check periodically to see if data has arrived. Some programs send emails or cards with status reports. Recommenders are notoriously lax in getting references in the pipeline, so be sure to check with the schools to see what is in and what is not. Do nudge to get things in.

Acceptances and Rejections

Acceptances

If you are accepted by several appealing programs, be sure to visit your first choice at least. When visiting, talk to students and see how they like the program and faculty. Also, talk to faculty in your area of interest to make sure they will be around for a while and how friendly they seem. Look carefully at financial aid and other benefits like health insurance. Get a sense of how students are regarded. Investigate the job placement success of recent graduates. Where are they working? Are they working in the field of study? If the vibes are bad at your first choice, visit your second. If you are going to be in a program three to five years, be sure it is a place where you can maximize your opportunities.

Rejections

What if you are rejected by every school? Find out why. Were they all "reaches"? Was the application pool especially large? Can you strengthen your application with better test scores, by taking more classes? Get some advice and then reapply.

How long should this go on? If you cannot get into any program in a certain field, consider trying another field. A neighbor's son tried for three years to get into medical school and finally switched successfully to law. Be realistic and persistent.

When you are working on applications also investigate external funding opportunities like those discussed in the next chapter.

Resources

Best Graduate Programs. Washington, D.C.: U.S. News & World Report.

Buskist, William, and Thomas R. Sherburne. *Preparing for Graduate Study in Psychology*. Boston: Allyn & Bacon, 1996.

Doughty, Harold. *Guide to American Graduate Schools*. New York: Viking Penguin, 1997.

Getting In: A Step-by-Step Plan to Gaining Admission to Graduate School in Psychology. Washington, D.C.: American Psychological Association, 1993.

Gourman, Jack. *Gourman Report of Graduate Programs: A Rating of Graduate and Professional Programs in American and International Universities*. New York: Princeton Review, 1997.

Graduate Study in Psychology. Washington, D.C.: American Psychological Association, 2002.

Hollis, Joseph. *Counselor Preparation: Programs, Faculty, Trends*. Bristol, Pa.: Accel Development, 1996.

Index of Majors and Graduate Degrees. New York: College Board.

Jerrard, Richard. *Graduate School Handbook: An Insider's Guide to Getting In and Succeeding*. New York: Berkley, 1998.

Montauk, Richard. *How to Get into Top MBA Programs*. Old Tappan, N.J.: Prentice-Hall, 1997.

Peterson's Guides. Princeton, N.J.: Peterson's Guides.

　Distance Learning Programs.
　Graduate Programs in Biological Sciences.
　Graduate Programs in Business, Education, Health, and Law.
　Graduate Programs in Education.

Graduate Programs in Engineering and Applied Sciences.
Graduate Programs in Humanities.
Graduate Programs in Physical Sciences.
Graduate Programs in Psychology.
Graduate Programs in Social Studies.
Graduate Schools in the U.S.: Explore Graduate and Professional Programs.
Independent Study Catalog: A Guide to Over Ten Thousand Correspondence Courses.
Princeton Review Guides to Testing. New York: Princeton Review.
Cracking the GMAT.
Cracking the GRE.
Cracking the GRE Biology.
Cracking the GRE Chemistry.
Cracking the GRE Literature.
Cracking the GRE Math.
Cracking the GRE Psychology.
Cracking the LSAT.
Cracking the MAT.
Cracking the MCAT.
Princeton Review Best Graduate Programs. New York: Princeton Review.
Engineering.
Humanities and the Social Sciences.
Physical and Biological Sciences.
Real Guide to Graduate School, Humanities. New York: Lingua Franca.
Real Guide to Graduate School, Social Sciences. New York: Lingua Franca.
Rold, Cynthia. *Real Life Guide to Graduate and Professional School.* Chapel Hill, N.C.: Pipeline Press, 1998.
Veterinary Medical School Admission Requirements. Association of Veterinary Medicine. West Lafayette, Ind.: Purdue University Press.

Chapter 2
External Funding

Graduate students receive most of their funding from their institution. University or internal funding is financial aid offered to applicants or enrolled students by or through the university to which they are applying or in which they are enrolled. In Chapter 1 we discussed various forms of university funding in detail.

Monies from outside the university, called external funds, include support from government agencies, private industry, and not-for-profits. Sometimes the distinctions between internal and external sources are not very clear. Training grants from the Department of Education called Graduate Assistance in the Areas of National Need are awarded to a department, and then the department recruits students who receive the funds. So the money is external but is filtered through the department. This type of fellowship is regarded as internal, not external.

For our purposes, *external funds* are those grants or fellowships that require you to fill out an application which is then sent directly to the agency. The university may facilitate the process and sign off on the application, but the student is the prime mover. It is common in the sciences to find students who have NSF or Howard Hughes fellowships, which are student initiated. In the social sciences and humanities, externally funded research grants, study abroad fellowships, and dissertation fellowships are typical. At times the award money is filtered through the institution, as with the Howard Hughes fellowships, but still the student filled out the application and is considered the awardee. Student credentials, programmatic quality, and institutional and student aggressiveness determine who wins outside awards.

With a few minor exceptions, the rest of this book will deal with external grants and fellowships for which you apply. We will find out what is available and how best to apply for them.

Over the years, two student groups have had more money made available for them than in the past. The first is minority and women students, who often have good funding sources at the master's and doctoral levels. People in any underrepresented category should be alert to these opportunities.

The second group includes those who study and do research abroad. Almost anyone with good foreign language skills and a good study/research plan should be able to find money from government or private sources. My son, for example, received funds that covered 50 percent of his costs to do research in Greece from the Explorers Club during his sophomore year in college.

If external money is not as readily available as internal funding, why bother? First- and second-year students who have portable training grants like those from the National Science Foundation or the Mellon Foundation can virtually pick the program they wish to attend. While it is not a guaranteed admission ticket, most programs will not turn away a student with three years of support.

Winning the first external award is important to winning future funding and is a wonderful job credential. In some fields, like the biomedical sciences or anthropology, success in grant writing is crucial for a researcher's future.

For doctoral students, nothing crystallizes the dissertation project like writing a grant proposal. The demands of grant writing, especially when done sometime after the dissertation proposal, can be an enormous help in further defining the project or getting it going again after a work-stop period.

Should you apply for a grant? See if it is the normal practice in your field. In medicine, for example, there is not much available in the way of training grants. But for those combining an M.D. with a Ph.D., the university and external funding picture is brighter.

Ph.D. students in every field should investigate external money. Research projects, especially those that require travel, usually have some agency interested in being of support. In my own case, in the field of social and cultural history, I won a sizable grant from the state to study the architecture of a rural county. My dissertation topic involved the study of a WPA building project, so the year I spent recording building styles for the state was beneficial both academically and financially.

Many external grants and fellowships require good test scores and high grade point averages, whereas others seek an arresting research project and strong faculty support. Belonging to a group that is underrepresented in your field (such as minorities and women) can be another important credential.

Where to Find Information About Grants and Fellowships

Many resources are geared toward helping students find money for graduate study and research. The best, most reliable, and current information is always found on the sponsoring agency's website, brochure, and application form. But other resources are also available to help find the agencies that are right for you.

Publications

The Resources section at the end of this chapter lists books published nationally. Some are directed to particular populations like minorities, women, scientists, and so on. The typical listing should give you enough information to determine whether the grant or fellowship is relevant to your interests.

The rest of the book lists the largest or most well-known external grant programs in all fields. Each listing has a great deal of information obtained from the agency that is not always available in their literature. The aim of the listings is to enable you to determine whether a try is reasonable and how best to write your application.

Where should you look for these publications? The main library is a good place to start. If there is a career center or career planning and placement office with a library, go there. Large universities may have a center devoted to helping students find external funding. Indiana University has such a center complete with staff who are of great assistance. Check with the graduate school to see if such a center exists.

Undergraduate deans' offices are often sources of information, as is the study abroad office.

An important source for federal funding is the *Catalog of Federal Domestic Assistance*, published by the government. The *Catalog* can be found in any major library. It is updated every six months and reflects the most current grants and fellowships available from every federal department and agency. The most up-to-date listing of funding is the *Federal Register*, but the *Catalog* is sufficiently current and comprehensive enough for most needs. The indexing is superb, and in most cases the grant descriptions give sample titles of the most recently funded proposals. The *Catalog* and the *Federal Register* are both online as well as in print.

Another good place to look for research money is in the *Encyclopedia of Associations*, which can be found in the reference section of most large libraries. This is good place to look for associations that offer grant money for research and tuition assistance. The listings usually include grant information.

Among other things the *Encyclopedia of Associations* lists ethnic organizations that offer support to students within their particular group. It also lists small scientific organizations that offer small grants.

Several publications, such as those issued by Peterson's, list grants for graduate students in general, and others, like the *Directory of Grants in the Humanities,* describe grants in specific fields.

Most states have an organization that houses funding resources and may publish a book of local and regional grants as well. These are good resources for local funding. Most grants available within a state are targeted to education, social welfare, health care, environment, conservation, or agriculture.

State agencies are also important sources of research money, especially for the social and agricultural sciences. Most state governments publish a book or website list of state agencies, their missions, and grants awarded. The Secretary of State's office and the state library are good places to look for agency information.

Computerized Searches

Internet searching for grants and fellowships has improved dramatically in the past few years. IRIS, for example, based at the University of Illinois, has been in business since the 1980s and is a great search engine, especially for research grants. Membership is required to utilize the IRIS database. Most universities make this connection available to graduate students through the graduate school.

Many universities also have online lists of grants and fellowships with direct links to the funding sources.

You should never rely solely on the Internet search. Start with the printed sources first, then move to the Internet. Using a book is a quicker way to make a list which can then be pursued online. Go to the library, peruse the publications, then search the net.

Other Information Sources

Other information sources include departmental faculty and advanced graduate students. In departments where people are routinely applying for outside money, faculty are significant founts of information. This is especially true for young faculty. More senior people may be removed from the days of writing small start-up grants.

Advisement offices, libraries, departments, and departmental libraries often have information resources for student grant hunters. Students should pressure departments to hold regular workshops on finding money and writing proposals. Some campuses have administrators who spend a lot of time helping students find funds. These people are found in the graduate division or school, research office, undergraduate college, grant center, library, or career office.

Up-to-Date Information and Deadlines

The most current information is found in the published brochures, application packets, and websites of the actual funding agencies. Anything found in trade publications is generally out of date. This is not a problem when doing a preliminary search for good grants and fellowships. But deadlines and other matters may change and must be checked from year to year.

Some agencies change their topic interests from time to time so having the current data is crucial. This is true for federal, state, and local governmental agencies, especially in the health care and social welfare fields.

If a deadline is coming up and the application is not available online, or if the deadline is past, call the agency to see how quickly you can get an application or if they will accept it past the deadline. Some agencies will not accept even the letters of recommendation after the deadline, yet others are not so strict.

Grant programs that are smaller and have fewer applications may not be so fussy about deadlines. Before you give up or spend hours of fruitless work, get assurances about application deadlines.

Application Forms

Getting application forms is a lot easier now than in the past. Most applications can be either filled out online or downloaded and mailed to the agency. Quite often, however, paper versions are available and may be found in departmental and graduate dean offices. Just be sure that the application form you get is current. Sometimes the agency will leave last year's version on the website after the deadline is past. It is fine to download this version to see what it is like, but be sure to get the current form before applying.

Some competitions must be applied for through the college or university. The application may be online, but it must be processed through your school. This is true for Rhodes, Marshall, Fulbright, and other fellowships. The undergraduate or graduate school offices will know who orchestrates these opportunities.

Types of External Funding

It helps to understand the different types of grants and fellowships out there. This section gives concise descriptions of these types. Subsequent chapters will expand upon the information below with descriptions of specific grants and fellowships.

Individual Training Fellowships

The National Science Foundation, Jacob Javits, GEM, and Mellon fellowships are just a few examples of grants for which senior undergraduates and first-year graduate students may apply.

The awards usually cover tuition and include stipends for living expenses. They may be used at any accredited institution, which means they are portable. Multiple years of support are the rule with these awards.

Study and Research Abroad

Students are generally interested in study or research abroad at three points in their academic careers. The first is during their undergraduate years when they go abroad for a summer or one or two semesters during their junior year. In addition, many undergraduates are interested in pursuing study or research programs the year following graduation. If you want to study abroad, look into the Fulbright, Rotary, Rhodes, Marshall, and Churchill fellowships and other programs during the spring semester of your junior year. Students engaged in many areas of graduate study are also interested in study or research abroad and opportunities are abundant.

Starting early is crucial. Almost all colleges and universities have information about these programs. The potential for getting funded is good. More than nine hundred Fulbright Fellowships awarded every year, for example.

While exceptional academic credentials are required for the Rhodes, Marshall, and Churchill programs, this is not as true for the Rotary or Fulbright, where good language and ambassadorial skills and worthy projects can be just as important.

Small Research Grants

Small research grants are awarded to students at all levels in all programs. While they are more likely to be found in arts and sciences, it is not impossible to receive them in other fields. They fall into three categories:

Exploratory grants are meant to encourage the development of ideas. The research project is usually in the embryonic stages, and the money goes to support a preliminary survey, lab research, or beginning field work.

Ongoing research grants are a means to keep a project going. The preliminary work is done and more money is needed for further research.

Library research grants are offered by libraries and museums and encourage students to travel to collections for study. Many of the presidential libraries offer grants for travel to their archives. The American Museum of Natural History and the Smithsonian also offer grants for travel to their various collections. These grants may be for work in the United States or abroad.

Large Research Grants

Large research grants usually support advanced research. Often they require the collaboration of a faculty mentor, and the funds may be filtered through the university. Students in the sciences and social sciences are most likely to be interested in large grant opportunities.

Dissertation Fellowships

Dissertation fellowships are monies set aside to fund dissertation research and/or writing. The National Science Foundation offers a dissertation improvement grant to students in some fields. The American Association of University Women also offers dissertation fellowships.

Grants of this nature have a large range of purposes, including support for living expenses while doing research and writing domestically or abroad. The Fulbright-Hays Dissertation Fellowships, for example, provides funding for area studies outside the United States in non-Western countries. Money is also available to cover expenses incurred in research including the purchase or rental of equipment and copying and mailing of surveys. Dissertation grants and fellowships may be offered to large groups of people with little regard for topic. The Ford Foundation Dissertation Fellowships for Minorities is such a program. Other dissertation grants are subject oriented. The Harry Frank Guggenheim Fellowships support dissertation research in the areas of violence and aggression.

Grants for Underrepresented and Specially Defined Groups

Grants for underrepresented and specially defined groups are available to people of color and of certain ethnic backgrounds and women in science, for example. While African Americans, Hispanics, Native Americans, and women are the most highly targeted groups, they are not the only groups eligible for these programs.

Postdoctoral Fellowships

Postdoctoral fellowships have become more prevalent in recent years. The postdoc is a transitional period wedged between graduate school and a permanent job placement. People holding postdoctoral fellowships often complain they are neither student nor faculty. In this limbo, they are not eligible for the benefits of being a graduate student or a faculty member.

There are postdoctoral positions that are funded by the institution and there are portable postdoctoral fellowships. The portable versions are usually for people who need to improve their career position. Maybe they need to complete a book in order to better their chances for tenure. A postdoctoral grant to do research abroad from the Social Science Research Council could fill that role. See Chapter 7 for a listing of major postdoctoral grants and fellowships.

Grant and Fellowship Application Tips

General Advice

1. *Start early.* This is true for any grant or fellowship but especially true for study or research abroad. Since award announcements are usually not made until eight months or more after application, it is important to start the process way ahead of schedule. Smaller grants with semiannual deadlines do not need the lead time that the larger variety does, but it is important to have an idea about what is available and when the deadlines fall. Really organized students have figured out a grant proposal plan that extends down the road two or three years. They are usually the most successful.
2. *Consult knowledgeable people on campus about funding.* Be careful to seek out everyone you can think of, including faculty, other graduate students, administrators who work regularly with funding information. Someone will have good information about where to look for outside money or can indicate who on campus has more information.
3. *Be persistent.* Too often students give up the hunt quickly when information about grants is not easy to find or when their applications are rejected. Students looking for research money, especially, should keep an eye out for opportunities and keep applying. There

are times, however, when reason should win out over persistence. If you are in the last stages of writing your thesis or dissertation, being preoccupied with grant writing may delay completing your degree. It might be smarter, at that point, to take out a loan and finish.

4. *Do not count on one application.* In general, the more applications you file, the better the odds are you will win an award. Be aware that some agencies will let you accept only one award at a time.

5. *Be sure your credentials, study or research plan, and project fit an agency's criteria.* It is important to read carefully the application sections on eligibility and the field focus requirements. Sometimes the descriptions are unclear, and you should not hesitate to call the agency if you have any questions. Sometimes emails work, but the telephone is much better, especially if there is a question related to topic.

   Permanent residents should be particularly alert to citizenship requirements: the federal government is inconsistent about including or excluding permanent residents in grant/fellowship eligibility requirements.

6. *Deadlines are sometimes flexible and sometimes not.* The more applications there are for a grant or fellowship, the less flexible the deadline is likely to be. A surprising number of agencies will bend a deadline rule if the date was missed by only a week or two. Smaller grants for research projects may have less stringent deadlines. When in doubt, have a faculty mentor or university administrator call the organization to inquire about and possibly influence deadline flexibility.

   Be warned that some agencies are so concerned about deadlines that if every piece of information—including transcripts, recommendations, and test scores—is not in on a prescribed day, the entire application is rejected. Read the deadline information very closely. If everything must be in by a certain date, be sure to tell recommenders, the registrar, and anyone else who contributes to a completed application what the date is. Give them plenty of advance notice of the deadline, and follow up to make sure items are sent in on time.

7. *If anything about the grant or fellowship confuses you, call or email the agency for a clarification.* There are times when a brochure or application leaves many questions unanswered. Don't pester the agency, but do find out what you need to know.

8. *Call to see if you can add materials to the application after the deadline.* Strict agencies aside, most organizations will add new pieces of information beyond the basic requirements to an application prior to committee evaluation. If additions significantly strengthen an application be sure to forward them for inclusion. Written confirmation

of contacts abroad, for example, can be key to the success of a Fulbright-Hays application. Acceptance of an article or book for publication could help a research grant application. Be sure the new information reaches the agency before the evaluation period.

9. *Do not be discouraged by rejection.* Students often give up after the first rejection. This is particularly true for research grants. After getting a rejection ask yourself the following questions: Was your methodology unclear? Did you follow the directions closely enough? Could faculty support have been stronger? Would another agency be more interested in your work? Can the budget be reworked; could you ask for less money? Sometimes you will get an evaluation with a rejection. Sometimes you can contact the agency and get a copy of the evaluation. Always try. Faculty and administrators can be helpful in reviewing a rejection and offering suggestions. Much federal money is tied to annual budget appropriations and the following year may be a better time to apply. Students looking for dissertation support should consider reapplying to the same agency if it is allowed. As research progresses, the project may become more attractive and promising. One student I know succeeded in winning a nationally prominent dissertation fellowship on the third try.

10. *Try to find out the ratio of applications to awards.* This information is found in the following chapters for most of the awards described. This data gives a realistic picture of the probability of winning and can help you decide whether or not to apply. Let's say you are thinking about applying for a national fellowship that pays tuition and stipend support. If you find out there are 4,000 applications for 80 grants, as there can be for the Javits, logic says that only students with the highest tests scores and GPAs and the most glowing recommendations have a shot at success. If you have these credentials, application makes sense; if you do not ... it does not.

Some awards fall into a gray zone where it is not so apparent statistically whether application is logical. When in doubt, apply.

11. *Following directions scrupulously.* The biggest mistake people make is not to follow directions. If an agency wants methodology first, put it first.

Most reviewers are given a list of evaluation criteria that reflect application directions. Beside each criterion is a numerical value. If methodology is worth 20 points, and the reviewer has to search for methodology or it is not well explained, you lose up to 20 points. A proposal is no place for subtle nuances that might be missed.

If the application enumerates the criteria, your response should be structured exactly the same way. If the application wants to know whether "(iv) The applicant has made preparations to establish research contacts and affiliations abroad," you should have a response section called Contacts and Affiliations Abroad.

Following directions carefully dramatically improves your chances of winning. Not following directions ruins any hope of an award.

Reviewers of fellowship and grant applications are generally overworked and are trying to get a lot done in a short amount of time. Having sat in hotel rooms in Washington with hundreds of applications in front of me and two days to read them, I can tell you that an applicant who does not follow directions is viewed with great disdain. It is an easy thing to accomplish, but many people fail to do it.

12. *If there is a weakness in the application of any sort, address it.* Maybe you have a bad grade on your transcript. Explain what happened; do not dwell on it but clarify it. Maybe you lack sufficient language skills. Explain how you will overcome that problem. Anything that might cause concern should be demystified in an honest and forthright manner.

Proposal-Writing Advice

1. *Use the funding agency's terminology.* A proposal sounds like it fits an agency's criteria if its words (from either the brochure or the application) are appropriately replicated in the proposal. Using the same terminology is tantamount to both substantively and psychologically responding directly to application criteria or agency mission. The Guggenheim, for example, wants proposals for projects that increase "the understanding of the causes, manifestations, and control of violence, aggression, and dominance." So the applicant should incorporate these words into the proposal.

   This sounds simplistic, but so often an applicant will attach a previously written dissertation proposal to an application and not tailor the words to the agency mission. Reviewers can spot this in an instant and are put off by the lack of effort taken in addressing the particular agency's needs. Once you annoy a reviewer sufficiently, you lose the award.

2. *Do not use excessive disciplinary jargon; write clearly and simply.* Many applications are reviewed by people in unrelated fields. Excessive jargon may be confusing to a reviewer in another discipline and lower your score. A Fulbright applicant in anthropology with whom I once worked kept referring to the study animals by their Latin names; I advised her to call them "monkeys" once in a while so that non-anthropologist reviewers could better understand the

proposal. Many application packets will advise against the use of jargon, so read carefully.

3. *Avoid excessive verbiage.* Getting to the point in a clear, concise, and comprehensive manner will be heartily appreciated by agencies and reviewers. Never, never go beyond the space or number of pages specified. Reviewers will only think you are incapable of organizing your information.

4. *Put the research you describe within the context of the entire project.* If you are seeking funding for part but not all of the project, it is important that the part be framed within the context of the entire project. Reviewers will better understand how crucial the part is to the whole and what the significance of the entire project is.

5. *Indicate the contribution any research project will make to the field.* The most important research is the most likely to be funded, so a paragraph on significance should be included even if not called for in the application.

6. *Work closely with a campus advisor or faculty mentor when writing the proposal.* If you are applying for a campus-administrated grant or fellowship like a Fulbright, pay close attention to what the administrator has to say and have him or her review at least one draft before completing the final version. If you are engaged in research, work closely with your mentor.

7. *Be willing to redraft your proposal three or four times.* Patience and persistence produce an effective proposal.

8. *Have others read the proposal for content, style, and typos.* Faculty or the administrative advisor should read for content. Have a stickler for detail and grammar read for language structure and typos.

9. *Be willing to reorganize the proposal to fit different applications.* There is a propensity to want to make one proposal fit all grant applications. This is a terrible mistake. Any reviewer will instantly recognize the one proposal-fits-all strategy and be unimpressed by it. An agency must recognize a project as one it could own, so the research must be described in its terms and according to its standards. Reworking the project description is absolutely worth the effort.

10. *Never sound tentative.* Do not use phrases like "I might be interested in ...," "I think it is possible that ...," "there is a good chance that...." These words suggest lack of confidence, confusion about direction, insufficient evidence, and indecisiveness.

11. *Be crystal clear about methodology.* Methodology is a plan of action, your approach to a problem or area of study. It is the structure you will follow to get things done. For a training fellowship applicant it is the field selection, types of classes, and possible research

interests that will lead to a degree. For the study/research abroad student, methodology can include a list of contacts, research/ study institutions, archives, and so on, and how they will be utilized within a time frame. Methodology should reflect accepted practices within fields. Every application requires an explanation of how things are going to get done even if the directions do not explicitly demand it.

Getting Good References

1. *References should usually be written by people who can attest to your academic promise or ability.* The application will usually indicate the most appropriate references. Do not stray from these demands. In most cases recommenders are faculty, although there are times when an expert from outside the academy may be acceptable. Most agencies are not looking for character references unless they so specify. When using faculty references try to utilize full-time people with faculty rank of assistant, associate, or full professor. Their opinions carry more weight than part-time faculty, postdocs, or teaching assistants. Teaching assistants, especially, lack credibility because they are in training and are viewed as short on the experience needed to judge other people's academic prospects. Part-time instructors (often called adjuncts) are not usually the best option unless they are famous in their field.

2. *A reference should know the applicant and be willing to write supportively and enthusiastically.* Weak or negative references will kill an application's prospects. Lukewarm praise is not much good either. Be sure to ask if a reference is willing to write positively. If not, find someone else who will.

3. *Give a reference plenty of advance notice.* People who write references for students are usually besieged with requests, especially in the fall. If you give references a month to get a letter constructed and sent, the odds are the letter will be more carefully written.

4. *Give references enough written data upon which to base the recommendation.* Give them a copy of the proposal and a resume or vita. Undergraduates applying for Fulbright, Rhodes, and other national fellowships should be sure to make a list of every course taken with the recommender, the grades, and copies of papers written in those courses. Be sure the reference understands why winning the grant or fellowship is important to you. The more you give them, the better the reference will be and the sooner it will be written.

5. *Check periodically to make sure the letter has been written and sent.* Faculty

are notoriously absent-minded. It is important to remain visible until the letter is sent. If you are having trouble, appeal to a departmental administrator like a secretary to promote your case to the faculty member. If you are away from campus, a well-timed phone call or email can be effective. The squeaky wheel concept works.

Chapters 1 and 2 are introductions to the worlds of graduate school and internal and external funding. They offer advice to facilitate the selection of a graduate program and construction of applications for grants and fellowships. The following chapters will target specific funding opportunities available outside the university.

Resources

Assistantships and Graduate Fellowships in the Mathematical Sciences, 2000–2001. Providence, R.I.: American Mathematical Society.

Bauer, David G. *The "How To" Grants Manual.* Phoenix, Ariz.: Oryx Press, 1999.

Blum, Laurie. *Free Money for Graduate School: A Guide to More than One Thousand Grants and Scholarships for Graduate Study.* New York: Facts on File, 1996.

Carlson, Mim. *Winning Grants Step by Step: Support Centers of America's Complete Workbook for Planning, Developing, and Writing Successful Proposals.* San Francisco: Jossey-Bass, 1995.

Catalog of Federal Domestic Assistance. Washington, D.C.: Government Printing Office. Annual, with mid-year updates.

Directory of Grants in the Humanities. Phoenix, Ariz.: Oryx Press.

Directory of Research Grants. Phoenix, Ariz.: Oryx Press.

Ferguson, Jacqueline. *Grants for Special Education and Rehabilitation.* Alexandria, Va.: Capital Publishing, 1994.

Foundation Center Publications. New York: Foundation Center.
    Grants for Alcohol and Drug Abuse.
    Grants for Film, Media and Communications.
    Grants for Medical and Profession Health Education.
    Grants for Mental Health, Addictions and Crisis Services.
    Grants for Public Health and Diseases.
    Grants for Social and Political Science Programs.
    Grants for the Aging.
    Grant Index.

McWade, Patricia. *Financing Graduate School: How to Get Money for Your Master's or Ph.D.* Princeton, N.J.: Peterson's Guides, 1996.

Morrone, John, Victoria Vinton, and Anna Jardine. *Grants and Awards Available to American Writers.* New York: PEN American Center, 1998.

Shlachter, Gale. *How to Find Out About Financial Aid and Funding: A Guide to Print, Electronic, and Internet Resources Listing Scholarships, Fellowships, Loans, Grants.* El Dorado Hills, Calif.: Reference Service Press, 1998.

Student Financial Services. *Government Financial Aid Book: The Insider's Guide to State and Federal Government Grants and Loans.* 3rd ed. Lansing, Mich.: Perpetual Press, 1998.

Tureen, Edward. *Grant Seeker's Primer: A Guide to Applying for Federal and Corporate Grants.* Champaign, Ill.: Sagamore Publishing, 1999.

Chapter 3
Individual Training Fellowships

This chapter presents general information and application writing advice for individual training fellowships. It also describes in detail certain specific fellowship opportunities, namely:

1. Department of Defense National Defense Science and Engineering (DOD-NDSEG) Graduate Fellowships
2. Ford Foundation Predoctoral Fellowships for Minorities
3. GEM Ph.D. Engineering or Science Fellowships
4. Hispanic Scholarship Fund
5. Howard Hughes Fellowships in the Biological Sciences
6. Jacob K. Javits Fellowships for Arts, Humanities, and Social Sciences
7. Andrew W. Mellon Fellowships in the Humanistic Studies
8. NASA Graduate Student Researchers Program Fellowships
9. National Physical Science Consortium (NPSC) Graduate Fellowships in the Physical Sciences
10. National Science Foundation (NSF) Graduate Research Fellowships in Science, Engineering, Social Science
11. National Security Education Program David L. Boren Graduate Fellowships for Language and Area Studies
12. Paul and Daisy Soros Fellowships for New Americans

Fellowships in this chapter are of interest to junior and senior undergraduates and first- through fifth-year graduate students. These fellowships fund most fields, and master's and doctoral degree programs.

General Information

Grants that provide money to pay tuition and fees and offer stipends for living expenses, books, and supplies for the first years of graduate education are called *training fellowships*. Some training fellowships require an application from the university to the funding agency; others require that the application be submitted by the student. Fellowships awarded by direct student application are the focus of this chapter.

A lot of money for graduate student support is offered through training fellowships. Each year, for example, the National Science Foundation alone funds nine hundred new three- to five-year awards, each worth a cost of living stipend for twelve months of $20,500 and with additional money for tuition. These awards support graduate work in engineering, science, and social science.

The federal government is the single greatest provider of training fellowship money but not the only source. Private organizations also support students in the first years of their programs. If you want to apply for any training fellowships described in this chapter, you should remember to check the fellowship's administrative web site or telephone to obtain the most current information about deadlines and application availability. Between the writing and publication of this book, deadlines, stipend amounts, and application criteria may have changed.

The point of this book is to make you aware of fellowships, help you understand how each fellowship is constructed and to what population it is targeted, provide you with information by which you can easily access the agency, and give useful advice about how to fill out the application.

General Application Advice

1. *Read and reread the application and agency information again and again from beginning to end.* Analyze the underlying purpose of why the fellowship was created. Try to understand what sort of student the organization wants to support. Be very clear on the application requirements.
2. *If something is not clear on the application, connect with a campus representative or contact the agency for clarification.* Some applications leave areas murky. Administrators and faculty on campus who have worked with the agency are good sources for quick answers. Agencies offer the most reliable data about the nuts and bolts of the application process such as when awards will be announced, how funding is arranged once an award is made, if it is possible to defer an award for a year, and so on. Web sites often have sections with commonly asked questions and their answers. If more is needed, there is usually an email address to which inquiries may be addressed. If all that fails, call the agency.
3. *Agencies are looking for academically focused individuals who they believe will end up in careers in which they will contribute to the betterment of the*

discipline and/or society in general. The Jacob Javits fellowship, for example, is designed to draw the brightest students into academic research and teaching in humanities, social sciences, and the arts. When writing the proposal statement be as academically knowledgeable and focused as possible. Applications to undergraduate school often encourage cleverness or diversity of interest. The opposite is true in graduate school matters. Reviewers will be more convinced that you are motivated and enthusiastic about your field and committed to completing your degree if you demonstrate a solid intellectual grounding and, in the best of all worlds, can show subfield expertise. This is not always easy for senior students, who may have had no more than two years of study in a major. Agencies are trying, at the application stage, to predict which candidates have been the most motivated in their studies, and are likely to remain enthusiastic. Understanding an applicant's knowledge base is one way of predicting potential success.

Somewhere on the web site, brochure or application packet the fellowship's purpose will be stated. It is very important to respond to that stated purpose somewhere when filling out the application. If, for example, the purpose of the fellowship is to encourage students to enter college teaching, then you must respond honestly that to be a college professor is your absolute goal in life. It seems like simplistic advice, but it is amazing the number of applicants who do not respond to the purpose and leave the agency unsure about study/career goals.

4. *Every single component in the application is important.* Most of the fellowships in this category are highly competitive, especially the Hughes, Ford, Javits, Mellon, and NSF awards. Grades must be great, GREs impressive, statements written with thoughtful focus, and references glowing. Many of these items are under your control. Certainly you can work and rework the application statements and have them reviewed by faculty or administrative mentors. Finding the most appropriate references is crucial to success.

5. *If the application is submitted on paper, not online, make sure everything you have written is easy to read.* Reviewers are usually faced with a pile of applications to read in a short time, and anything that makes it difficult can be annoying. Type faces that are small, dark, and condensed should be avoided. If basic information is filled out by hand, print neatly.

6. *If an award is denied and reapplication is an option, ask the agency for reviewer's comments.* Many are willing to accommodate such requests; the few that do not will usually say so in their policy information.

Specific Fellowship Opportunities

The following fellowships include those that offer the largest number of awards and also represent a wide range of student interests from fine arts to engineering. Most are funded by the federal government. If the fellowship that interests you is not listed here, try the various resources listed at the end of Chapter 2.

All information herein, except the author's advice, is taken from the actual agency web site, brochure, and application packet or from telephone calls or emails to the agencies. Every effort has been made to use the agency language or to paraphrase or summarize that language. For ease of reading, quotation marks are only used to draw special attention to important sections.

1. Department of Defense National Defense Science and Engineering Graduate Fellowships (DOD-NDSEG)

(Based on 2002–2003 NDSEG Fellowships)
Administrative Agency: American Society for Engineering Education
Address: American Society for Engineering Education
      1818 N Street, NW, Suite 600
      Washington, DC 20036
      Attn: NDSEG Program Manager
      Phone: 202-331-3516; fax: 202-265-8504
      Email: ndseg@asee.org
      Web: www.asee.org/ndseg
Deadline and Notification: Mid-January application deadline; 70–90 days for award notification.
Number of Awards: 150–275 per competition depending on available funding. There were 148 in 1999, 108 in 2000, and 285 in 2001.
Average Number of Applicants: The total number of applicants for 1996 through 2000 was 6,147, with an average of 9.1 percent being funded. Each field is different. In chemical engineering, 3.8 percent of applicants received awards, while 28.4 percent in ocean engineering received awards. In the past twelve years, 25,200 applications were received and 1,300 fellowships were awarded. The application supplies "chances of winning" stats for all fields.
Other Related Fellowships: NSF and GEM fellowships.
Award Amount: 2001–2002 stipend is $19,000; 2002–2003 is $20,000; 2003–2004 is $21,000 for a twelve-month academic year. Also, tuition and fees are paid to the awardee's university. Additional allowances may be available to people with disabilities.

Application Form: Science departments, dean's office, graduate school office, career center; or write to the above address. As of this writing the application is not available online.

Purpose of Grant/Fellowship and Restrictions: The object is to support doctoral students in: aeronautical and astronautical engineering; biosciences (including toxicology); chemical engineering; chemistry; cognitive, neural and behavior sciences; computer science; electrical engineering; geosciences (including terrain, water, and air); materials science and engineering; mathematics; mechanical engineering; naval architecture and ocean engineering; physics (includes optics); manufacturing sciences and engineering; and nanotechnology. The basic goal is to train American men and women in disciplines that have the greatest payoff for national security. There is no obligation to serve the government if this award is won.

Length of Award: Three years (12 months per year).

Applicant Eligibility: U.S. citizens or U.S nationals. This does not include permanent residents. Current senior college students and first-year graduate students and those who have received a bachelor's degree but not started graduate school. Students changing fields in the early stages of graduate school with some restrictions.

Application Requirements: Personal information forms; official transcripts; three references; general GRE test results.

Application Comments and Advice: The program is looking for independent, creative thinkers who can present their educational goals and objectives thoughtfully and concisely. The educational plan needs to be presented in a specific, focused, and concise manner, much like the description of a compelling research project. It is important to have your references read your statements before they write any recommendations: first, for their criticisms, and second, so that every part of the application fits together. Be sure to read the Detailed Instruction section very carefully.

2. Ford Foundation Predoctoral Fellowships for Minorities

(Based on 2002–2003 Fellowships)

Administrative Agency: National Research Council

Address: National Research Council
        Fellowship Programs Office/FF, TJ 2041
        2001 Wisconsin Avenue, NW
        Washington, DC 20007
        Phone: 202-334-2872; fax: 202-334-3419
        Email: infofell@nas.edu
        Web: http://national-academies.org/fellowships

Deadline and Notification: Early November deadline; April award notification.

Number of Awards: 60 per competition.

Average Number of Applicants: 800–1,000 per competition.

Other Related Fellowships: NSF, GEM, Hughes NSEP fellowships.

Award Amount: Annual stipend of $16,000 plus allowance for tuition and fees. Three years of support, which must be used within five years. Expenses to attend conferences for fellows.

Application Form: Application may be completed online or may be requested from the above address.

Purpose of Grant/Fellowship and Restrictions: To increase the presence of underrepresented minorities on college and university faculties. Minority groups are Alaskan natives; Black/African Americans; Mexican Americans; Native American Indians; Native Pacific Islanders; and Puerto Ricans.

Length of Award: Three years.

Applicant Eligibility: Citizens or nationals of the United States. Not permanent residents. Membership in one of the above minority groups. Enrollment in or planned enrollment in a research-based Ph.D. or Sc.D. program. Most arts and sciences and engineering fields are acceptable, but check the areas listed on the application. Undergraduate seniors; first-year graduate students; students who have a bachelor's degree but are not enrolled in graduate school.

Application Requirements: Completed application form; four references; GRE test results; all transcripts.

Application Comments and Advice: Enthusiasm for college teaching, university research, and academia in general must be communicated as the ultimate goal. Helping other underrepresented minorities to become interested in an academic career is also an aim of the program and should be addressed. Be sure that the programs to which you have applied are the best suited to your graduate plan because the reviewers are interested in that aspect.

3. GEM Ph.D. Engineering or Science Fellowships

(Based 2002–2003 Fellowships)

Administrative Agency: National Consortium for Graduate Degrees for Minorities

Address: GEM Ph.D. Science Fellowship Program
       Box 537
       Notre Dame, IN 46556
       Phone: 219-631-7771

Email: gem.1@nd.edu

Web: www.nd.edu/~gem

Deadline and Notification: December 1 deadline; notification of award in February.

Number of Awards: 200 master's; 30 Ph.D., per competition.

Average Number of Applicants: 500–600 per competition.

Other Related Fellowships: NSF, Ford, Hughes fellowships.

Award Amount: $12,000 per year plus tuition and fees.

Application Form: Can be completed online or requested from the above address.

Purpose of Grant/Fellowship and Restrictions: To encourage minorities to pursue master's and doctoral programs in science and engineering at specific universities that are members of the GEM consortium. That list is provided on the web site and includes most major universities. Minority groups include: American Indians; African Americans; Mexican Americans; Puerto Ricans and other Hispanic American groups.

Length of Award: Master's students are supported three semesters; Ph.D.s for the first academic year by GEM and then by the awardee's university.

Applicant Eligibility: U.S. citizens and members of minority groups listed above who have applied to at least three of the fifty National Consortium member universities. GPA of 3.0 or better on a 4.0 scale.

Application Requirements: Completed application; all transcripts; one-page resume for doctoral students. Application to three GEM member universities for seniors or bachelor's recipients.

Application Comments and Advice: The application is relatively modest in requirements. Be sure to have applied to three GEM schools. These schools may be found on the GEM web site. All students must intern with a GEM corporate member after their first year, and company preferences should be listed. There is a list of corporate members of the consortium on the web site. The internship is supported financially by the fellowship. Researching the corporate internships before application is very important.

4. Hispanic Scholarship Fund

(Based on 2001–2002 Scholarships)

Administrative Agency: Hispanic Scholarship Fund

Address: Hispanic Scholarship Fund
One Sansome Street, Suite 1000
San Francisco, CA 94104
Phone: 877-473-4636

Email: info@hsf.net
Web: www.hsf.net

Deadline: October 15.

Other Related Scholarships: Ford, GEM fellowships.

Award Amount: $1,000–$3,000.

Application Form: Available from the website August 1 to October 15, or send a stamped, business size, self-addressed envelope to the above address.

Purpose of Scholarship and Restrictions: To help college and university students at all levels complete their education.

Applicant Eligibility: At least half Hispanic ancestry, with one parent fully Hispanic or both half-Hispanic. U.S. citizen or permanent resident. Attending a fully accredited university full-time. Cumulative GPA of 2.7 or better.

Application Requirements: Transcripts which show cumulative grade point average; one letter of recommendation from a college or university faculty or administrator; personal statement; copy of financial aid history.

Application Comments and Advice: The personal statement requires a family tree that indicates Hispanic heritage of at least 50 percent. Of real importance in the statement is your commitment in the past, present, and future to making a difference in your community. Since the idea is to facilitate degree completion, be sure to include a convincing plan that includes a time frame for degree completion. All pieces of information for the application should be included in one packet and then sent to the agency. Selection is based on academic achievement, the strength of the letter of recommendation, the quality of the personal statement, and financial need. Be sure to seek out the best academic recommendation possible.

5. Howard Hughes Fellowships in Biological Sciences

(Based on 2002–2003 Fellowships)

Administrative Agency: National Research Council

Address: Hughes Predoctoral Fellowships
Fellowship Office
National Research Council
2001 Wisconsin Avenue, NW
Washington, DC 20007
Phone: 202-334-2872; fax: 202-334-3419
Email: infofell@nas.edu
Web: http://national-academies.org/fellowships

Deadline: Application early November; April for award notification.

Number of Awards: 80 predoctoral fellowships per competition.

Average Number of Applicants: 1,100 per competition.

Award Amount: $21,000 stipend per year plus tuition and fees allowance.

Other Related Awards: NSF, Ford, GEM fellowships.

Application Form: Online application through the above web site.

Purpose of Grant/Fellowship and Restrictions: To support doctoral students to pursue degrees in biomedical research in: biochemistry; bioformatics; biophysics; biostatistics; cell biology; developmental biology; epidemiology; genetics; immunology; mathematical and computational biology; microbiology; molecular biology; neuroscience; pharmacology; physiology; structural biology; virology.

Length of Award: Five years.

Applicant Eligibility: Students in or near the beginning of their graduate work in the above fields; no citizenship requirement.

Application Requirements: Completed application in English; four references from faculty who can comment on current academic and scientific abilities; general GRE test scores and relevant subject score; all academic transcripts.

Application Comments and Advice: Read the agency's application tips carefully. The proposed plan of research and study section may not be a rehash of your bachelor thesis but must be a new project with a "clearly stated testable hypothesis." It is the scientific process that should be emphasized, not the scientific minutia. In the educational objectives section remember that the idea is to support future researchers so think and write about your goals beyond graduate school. This program is looking for top students who have a big vision when approaching important scientific questions. All sections of the application should work as a whole and should avoid repetition. Your goals, previous research experience, proposed plan of research/study and references should all be integrated like parts of a symphony. To this end, it is important that recommenders see a draft of the application before writing references or at least have a sense of how you will approach the proposal.

6. Jacob K. Javits Fellowships for the Arts, Humanities, and Social Sciences

(Based on 2002–2003 Fellowships)

Administrative Agency: U.S. Department of Education

Address: Jacob K. Javits Fellowship Program
Department of Education
1990 K Street, NW, Suite 6000
Washington, DC 20006-8521

Phone: 202-502-7700; fax: 301-470-1244

Email: ope_javits_program@ed.gov

Web: www.ed.gov/offices/OPE/HEP/iegps/javits.html for application and general information.

Deadline and Notification: November for application; early March for award notification.

Number of Awards: Number of awards depends on yearly government appropriations. For 2000, 162 new awards and 260 continuing; for 2001, 42 new awards and 317 continuing; for 2002, 94 new awards and 341 continuing.

Other Related Awards: Mellon, Ford, National Security Education fellowships.

Average Number of Applicants: 2,500–3,000 per competition.

Award Amount: $18,000 plus tuition and fees.

Application Form: Apply online or order application by mail or email from above address.

Purpose of Grant/Fellowship and Restrictions: To support graduate study at the doctoral or M.F.A. level in the following fields: *Arts:* art and architectural history; creative writing; music performance, theory, composition, and literature; studio arts; television, film, and cinematography; theatre arts, play writing, screen writing, acting, and dance. *Humanities:* archaeology; area studies; classics; comparative literature; English language and literature; folklore, folk life; foreign languages and literature; history; linguistics; philosophy; religion (not for divinity school); speech, rhetoric, and debate. *Social Sciences:* anthropology; communications and media; economics; ethnic and cultural studies; political science; public policy, and public administration; sociology.

Length of Award: Up to four years.

Applicant Eligibility: Students who are about to begin or near the beginning of a doctoral or M.F.A. program in one of the above fields with at least 60 percent of awards going to applicants with no graduate credits. U.S. citizen, U.S. national, permanent residents, or citizens of a Freely Associated State.

Application Requirements: Completed application; GRE test scores for doctoral and some M.F.A. applicants; all transcripts; three letters of recommendation; skill demonstration materials for M.F.A. students with strict submission rules.

Application Comments and Advice: Division of the awards is as follows: 60 percent to the humanities; 20 percent to the arts; 20 percent to the social sciences. In addition, 60 percent of the awards go to students with no graduate credit, so this grant really favors humanities majors who have not yet started a graduate program.

The Javits material contains a section explaining how the 400 or less review points are awarded, which should help you decide whether to apply for this award. I was a reader for this fellowship and can tell you that because of the volume of applications you will probably need a score or 385 or better out of 400 to be in the final cut.

Realistically, in the doctoral section, you need almost perfect grades and top GRE scores to have any chance of success. If grades and scores are a real weakness, do not bother with this application unless you can explain the weakness. Maybe you were sick (in which case a reference needs to testify to this). If everything else is superlative, then a weakness in grades and tests may be overcome, but it is extremely difficult to do. The emphasis on grades is 50 points less in the arts, where is greater emphasis on creativity.

Everything counts, so this application needs lots of time and care in preparation. References need to be terrific and should be from full-time, high-ranking faculty who know your work best.

7. Andrew W. Mellon Fellowships in the Humanistic Studies

(Based on 2002–2003 Fellowships)
Administrative Agency: Woodrow Wilson Foundation
Address: Andrew W. Mellon Fellowships in the Humanistic Studies
　　　Woodrow Wilson Foundation
　　　CN 5281
　　　Princeton, NJ 08543-5281
　　　Phone: 609-452-7007; fax: 609-452-0066
　　　Email: mellon@woodrow.org
　　　Web: www.woodrow.org/mellon/
Deadline and Notification: Mid-December for application; interviews in March; early April award notification.
Number of Awards: 85 per competition.
Average Number of Applicants: 800 per competition.
Other Related Awards: Ford, Javits, National Security Education fellowships.
Award Amount: $17,500 stipend for one academic year plus tuition and fees.
Application Form: Online application from web site above.
Purpose of Grant/Fellowship and Restrictions: To support exceptional doctoral students who aim for careers in college and university teaching and research in the humanistic studies of the following fields: art history; classics; comparative literature; critical theory; cultural anthropology, cultural studies including all area studies; English literature; ethnic studies; ethnomusicology; foreign language and literature; history; history and philosophy of mathematics; history and philosophy

of science; humanities; interdisciplinary studies; cultural linguistics; music history and theory; political philosophy; political theory; religion/religious studies; rhetoric; women's studies.

Length of Award: One year.

Applicant Eligibility: U.S. citizen or permanent resident; college senior or graduate who has not yet enrolled in graduate school. Selection of a humanities course of study listed above. With some exceptions, the program should be at the doctoral level. Applicants who have done graduate work in one field should be enrolling in a program in another field. If this is unclear, be sure to call the agency for clarification.

Application Requirements: A completed online application; GRE test scores; all transcripts; three references; writing sample; statement of interest.

Application Comments and Advice: The foundation's Guide to Application makes very clear what is acceptable and what is not. This is described as a very formal process. Since they are seeking academic professionals, this is the time to be very careful about spelling, syntax, and grammar.

Students who make the first cut will be invited to interview in March. Consult with someone on your campus, perhaps in the career center or, preferably, with a faculty member who has had a Mellon, about how to prepare for an interview. Another source on campus for interviewing strategies is the administrator who oversees the Rhodes, Marshall, and Fulbright competitions. All have an interview component.

If you read the application carefully and follow the directions to the letter you will have the best opportunity for success.

8. NASA Graduate Student Researchers Program Fellowships

(Based on 2002–2003 Fellowships)

Administrative Agency: NASA

Address: NASA GSRP
        National Program Manager
        Office of Human Resources and Education
        Code FE
        NASA Headquarters
        Washington, DC 20546
        Phone: 202-358-0402; fax: 202-358-3048
        Email: kblandin@hq.nasa.gov
        Web: http://education.nasa.gov/gsrp/admin.html

Deadline and Notification: Early February for application submission. Early May for award notification.

Number of Awards: 90–160 per competition, depending upon appropriations.

Other Related Fellowships: DOD-NDSEG, Ford, GEM, NPSC, NSEP fellowships.

Award Amount: $24,000 maximum includes stipend plus some money for tuition and fees and travel to laboratories.

Application Form: Can be accessed online but must be returned with multiple copies to selected research centers.

Purpose of Grant/Fellowship and Restrictions: The purpose is to facilitate the training of highly qualified personnel for careers in aerospace, space science, space applications, space technology. This fellowship is available to students seeking master's and doctoral degrees in the following fields: astronomy; atmospheric sciences; biological sciences; chemistry; computer science; environmental sciences; geology; life sciences; mathematics; oceanography; physics; physical sciences; psychology; social sciences.

Students are funded to take courses at their universities and to also conduct research at one of the NASA facilities (less time is spent at headquarters than the other sites) which include: NASA Headquarters (3 programs); Ames Research Center; Dryden Research Center; Glenn Research Center; Goddard Space Flight Center; Jet Propulsion Laboratory; Johnson Space Center; Kennedy Space Center; Langley Research Center; Marshall Space Center; Stennis Space Center.

Length of Award: One to three years.

Applicant Eligibility: U.S. citizens. Seniors in college or students already enrolled in master's or doctoral programs in science, engineering and social science. Applicants must have a faculty sponsor. Minority group members and women are encouraged to apply.

Application Requirements: Completed application; faculty sponsor recommendation; all transcripts.

Application Comments and Advice: The proposal requires contact with the NASA facility where the research is to take place and requires collaboration with a faculty member at the university. This means lots of planning and much consultation with a faculty member willing to sponsor your project. The application also requires numerous sheets to be signed by university officials and this can require time, so start early.

9. National Physical Science Consortium Graduate Fellowships in the Physical Sciences (NPSC)

(Based on 2002–2003 Fellowships)

Administrative Agency: National Physical Science Consortium

Address: National Physical Science Consortium
MSC-3NPS

Student Recruitment Office
New Mexico State University
Box 30001
Las Cruces, NM 88003-8001
Phone: 800-952-4118 or 505-646-6038; fax: 505-646-6097
Email: npsc@npsc.org
Web: www.npsc.org

Deadline and Notification: Early November for application submission. Award notification in late January or early February.

Number of Awards: 22 per competition.

Average Number of Applicants: 200–250 per competition.

Other Related Awards: Ford, GEM, NSF, NSEP fellowships.

Award Amount: $12,500 stipend for years one through four; $15,000 stipend for years five and six. Tuition and fees are paid by university attended. Two summer internships at consortium employers are paid by the employer and include round-trip transportation allowance.

Application Form: Online from the above web site.

Purpose of Grant/Fellowship and Restrictions: To support full-time doctoral graduate work in the physical sciences and related engineering fields which include: astronomy; chemistry; computer science; geology; materials science; mathematical sciences; physics; engineering fields, including chemical, computer, electrical, environmental, and mechanical engineering.

Special emphasis is on the recruitment of underrepresented groups, especially minorities and women. Minority groups emphasized include: African-American; Hispanic; Native American Indian; Eskimo; Aleut; Pacific Islander (Polynesian), and/or females.

Length of Award: Four years, renewable up to six years.

Applicant Eligibility: U.S. citizen. Undergraduate GPA of 3.0 out of 4.0. Graduating seniors; M.A. students at non-Ph.D. granting institutions; applicants with bachelor's degrees who have been out of school for a year or more. Must be eligible to study at a participating National Physical Science Consortium university. A complete list of schools is available on the web site and includes most research universities with doctoral programs in the physical sciences and engineering.

Application Requirements: Completed application form; GRE test scores; three to five references. Form is filled in online then printed, signed, and mailed to the consortium. The web site has very good instructions for filling out the application.

Application Comments and Advice: This is a very straightforward application with minimal requirements. You must list the Consortium universities to which you have and/or intend to apply. You must also list the Consortium corporate partners for which you would be willing to work the summers prior to and following your first year in graduate school. The corporate partners list can be accessed on the web site. You should research these partners carefully before indicating which would be the most desirable places to work. The work element is a very important component of this fellowship, as it is with the GEM program.

The primary criteria for selecting fellows includes: academic standing; quality of course work taken relative to proposed graduate work; research experience; letters of recommendation.

10. National Science Foundation Graduate Research Fellowships in Science, Engineering, and Social Science (NSF)

(Based on 2002–2003 Fellowships)

Administrative Agency: National Science Foundation

Address: NSF Graduate Research Fellowship Program
      Oak Ridge Associated Universities
      PO Box 3010
      Oak Ridge, TN 37831-3010
      Phone: 865-241-4300; fax: 865-241-4513
      Email: nsfgrfp@orau.gov
      Web: www.orau.org/nsf/nsffel.htm
      For online submission help: 800-673-6188 or fellapp@nsf.gov

Deadline and Notification: Early November for application; March for award announcement.

Number of Awards: 900 per competition.

Average Number of Applicants: 5,500 per competition.

Other Related Awards: Ford, GEM, Hughes, Javits fellowships.

Award Amount: $20,500 stipend for 12 months with allowance for tuition and fees, and travel.

Application Form: Online application available at: www.fastlane.nsf.gov. Applicants are expected to use the online application, but if they have no access to a computer, they may use the postal service. No application may be faxed or emailed.

Purpose of Grant/Fellowship and Restrictions: To support doctoral students in science, engineering, and social sciences and to encourage diversity in those fields. The fields include a broad range of disciplines in the following areas: chemistry; computer and information science and engineering; engineering; geosciences; life sciences; mathematical sciences; physics and astronomy; psychology; social sciences; science education. Support is not offered for any practice-oriented professional degree program such as an M.D./Ph.D. or J.D./Ph.D.

Length of Award: Three years of support, which may be used over a period of five years.

Applicant Eligibility: U.S. citizens, U.S. nationals, permanent residents of the United States; seniors in college, students in their first year of graduate school, students at the beginning of their second year. All must be applying to or enrolled in a doctoral program in a discipline from one of the fields listed above. The NSF information site lists all the acceptable programs.

Application Requirements: Completed application; all transcripts; four references; GRE test scores. Application must be done online unless no computer is available.

Application Comments and Advice: The "Instructions for Completing a Fellowship Application" is full of good advice. That section is in the booklet which should be available in science departments, engineering schools, graduate school offices, and some career centers. Read the instructions very carefully and work closely with your advisor. Four sections, which include #16 Personal and Education Experiences, #17 Integrating Research and Education, Proposed Plan of Research, and Previous Research Experience, should be viewed as parts of a whole. While it is important to tie these sections together, candidates should be careful not to be repetitious and should present new information in each area. That new information could connect to the other sections and perhaps be an elaboration of something mentioned elsewhere. A Proposed Research Plan may have had its origins in another grant proposal's Previous Research Experience or a Personal or Educational Experience.

Being able to demonstrate a vision of the big picture yet incorporate specific disciplinary principles is important.

11. National Security Educational Program
David L. Boren Graduate Fellowships for Language and Area Studies (NSEP)

(Based on 2002–2003 Fellowships)
Administrative Agency: Academy for Educational Development
Address: Academy for Educational Development
       1825 Connecticut Avenue, NW
       Washington, DC 20009-5721
       Phone: 800-498-9360 or 202-884-8285; fax: 202-884-8407
       Email: nsep@aed.org
       Web: www.aed.org/nsep
Deadline and Notification: February 1 for application submission; late April for award announcements.
Number of Awards: 90–100 per competition.
Average Number of Applicants: 350–400 per competition.

Other Related Awards: Javits, GEM, Ford, Fulbright, Rotary fellowships.

Award Amount: For domestic language or area studies course work: $2,000 a semester, not to exceed $12,000 for up to six semesters of study. For overseas study: $10,000 for up to two terms not to exceed $20,000. No more than $28,000 for a combined overseas and domestic study program.

Application Form: Available online from the above web address or by mail from the above postal address or by email request.

Purpose of Grant/Fellowship and Restrictions: The mission is to support language and area studies relating to eighty annually selected countries and forty-five languages. Not supported are language study and research in Western European countries, Canada, Australia, or New Zealand. The idea is to promote study in languages and areas which are underrepresented.

The selected countries are tied to the President's annual National Security Strategy. And while security is of utmost import, this fellowship also supports study in the areas of sustainable development, environmental degradation, global disease and hunger, population growth and migration, and economic competitiveness. Acceptable fields of study include: agriculture and food sciences; business and economics; computer and information sciences; engineering and applied sciences in the areas of: biology; chemistry; environmental sciences; mathematics; physics; health and biomedical sciences; history; international affairs; law; political science and policy studies; and other social sciences including anthropology, psychology, and sociology.

Length of Award: Up to six semesters for language study; up to two semesters for overseas study.

Applicant Eligibility: U.S. citizen. Enrollment in a U.S. graduate degree program or acceptance into such a program. Graduate degrees pursued include master's as well as a variety of doctoral and professional degrees such as M.D., Ph.D., J.D., and Sc.D. Willingness to fulfill a service requirement with the U.S. government.

Service Requirement: Within five years of graduation, awardees must begin service in a federal or independent agency or office. Service is tied to award duration but is usually not less than a year. These entities include: Department of Commerce; Department of Defense; Department of Energy; Department of Justice; Department of State; Department of Treasury; U.S. Intelligence; National Security Council; Office of Budget and Management; Office of National Drug Control Policy; Office of Science and Technology; Office of the U.S. Trade Representative; United States Congress Committee Staffs, Research Service; Agency for International Development; Export-Import Bank of the U.S.; U.S. International Trade Commission.

If a good-faith effort at gaining employment at one of the above is unsuccessful, awardees may repay the fellowship by working in higher education in the field of study.

Application Requirements: Application completed online or on hard copy; all transcripts; service agreement form; three letters of reference; language evaluation form.

Application Comments and Advice: This application takes a great deal of thought. The objectives of the program are clearly stated but not so easily fulfilled. First, this program is looking for applicants who are committed to working in U.S. government or federally related organizations in positions which enhance national security. Relating such career goals enthusiastically is therefore important.

Next, you must describe why the area you have chosen is crucial to your research as well as in the national interest, what your specific project is, and how you are going to implement your proposed plan. This fellowship requires a very specific road map of your educational plan. Be sure to research the country you are going to study and the specific classes you will take to enhance this knowledge. Have a very clear time line which includes language classes and any overseas travel.

The application gives a list of sample programs that include: "An M.B.A. student from Brigham Young studying Bulgarian, and examining microenterprise and microcredit organizations in Bulgaria" and "A Ph.D. student from Columbia University studying Zulu and Swahili, and conducting research on South African policies on arms production, sales, and procurement." These should serve as good indicators of the sorts of projects that are funded.

If you have a Fulbright officer on your campus, you might try to speak to him or her about how to structure your application, as the overseas component is similar to that of a research Fulbright. Fulbright campus committees include members of the faculty from a wide spectrum of departments, and one of them might also be a good source of information and help with your application.

For applicants in professional schools, find a faculty member who has done research in non-Western countries for a realistic assessment of what it takes to work in a non-Western climate.

Remember that any overseas project must be feasible. The final piece of advice on overseas projects is to establish contacts in the country in which you propose to do research. If you are going to study a specific disease, for example, you must have found a clinic and a contact where that disease is being treated, and that place must be willing to provide access to the patient population. The more remote the geographic location, the more important the contacts.

12. Paul and Daisy Soros Fellowships for New Americans

(Based on 2002–2003 Fellowships)

Administrative Agency: Paul and Daisy Soros Fellowships for New Americans

Address: 400 West 59th Street
New York, NY 10019
Phone: 212-547-6926; fax: 212-548-4623
Email: pdsoros_fellows@sorosny.org
Web: www.pdsoros.org

Deadline and Notification: November 30 for application submission; early March award notification.

Number of Awards: 30 per competition.

Average Number of Applicants: 875 average per competition over four years; in 2001 there were 933 applicants.

Award Amount: $20,000 stipend plus half of tuition costs.

Application Form: Available online from the above website.

Purpose of Grant/Fellowship and Restrictions: This grant supports new Americans, defined as resident aliens, naturalized citizens, or the children of naturalized citizens, in any professional or scholarly graduate program. The Soros trust is looking for new Americans who are devoted to their or their parents' new country and who will be important contributors to the culture and society of the United States.

College graduates who have not attended graduate school are strongly supported, but consideration is given first to first- or second-year graduate students. In 2001 there were 102 fellows studying at thirty universities in twenty-six graduate subjects. Fellows must enroll at an accredited graduate program in the United States. Applicants must be loyal and committed to the United States and consider it their principal residence and focus of national identity.

Length of Award: Two years.

Applicant Eligibility: Permanent resident; naturalized citizen or child of two parents who are both naturalized citizens. Evidence of two of the following: (1) demonstrated creativity, originality, initiative; (2) a commitment to and capacity for accomplishment demonstrated through activity that has required drive and sustained effort; (3) commitment to the values expressed in the U.S. Constitution and the Bill of Rights, including activity that supports human rights and the rule of law and in advancing the responsibilities of citizenship in a free society.

Application Requirements: A completed application with complete citizenship information; test scores; two essays; two references.

Application Comments and Advice: The first essay asks you to describe your experiences as a new American. Emphasis is on how family and experiences contributed to being an American. In addition, you are asked to give evidence of your creativity, accomplishments, and commitment to the values found in the U.S. Constitution and the Bill of Rights.

The best approach is to weave the experiences into creativity, accomplishments, and documentary values. For example, perhaps the experience of becoming a citizen or obtaining a green card resulted in a profound interest and respect for the Bill of Rights. The Bill of Rights might be so different from the values of your homeland (or your parents') that you were inspired to speak of these contrasts to groups like the Rotary Club. Any essay should be filled with substantive, detailed examples that support your values and ideals.

The second essay is a statement about educational and career goals and objectives. If it makes sense, tie your goals and objectives to the experiences and values described in the first essay.

Eighty-four finalists are interviewed. Commitment to the values of the United States is an important quality to communicate during this process. Be sure to talk to an advisor on your campus about interviewing. The Fulbright or Mellon fellowship advisor is a good source of information.

Chapter 4
Study and Research Abroad

This chapter presents general information and application writing advice for study/research abroad fellowships. It also describes in detail certain specific fellowship opportunities, namely:

1. British Marshall Scholarships
2. Deutscher Akademischer AustauschDienst Grants (DAAD) for Study and Research in Germany
3. Fulbright (IIE) Grants for Graduate Study, Research, and Teaching Abroad
4. Fulbright-Hays Doctoral Dissertation Research Abroad Program
5. International Research and Exchange Board (IREX) Grants for Central and Eastern Europe, Eurasia, Mongolia, Turkey, Iran
6. Japanese Government Monbusho Scholarships for Language and Culture Study and for Research
7. National Security Education Program David L. Boren Graduate Fellowships for Language and Area Studies (NSEP)
8. Rhodes Scholarships for Study at Oxford University
9. Rotary Academic Year, Multi-Year, and Cultural Ambassadorial Scholarships
10. Social Science Research Council (SSRC) International Predissertation Fellowships; Fellowships for the Study of the Russian Empire, the Soviet Union, and Its Successor States; Predissertation Fellowships for Bangladesh

Fellowships in this section are of interest to junior and senior undergraduates and first- through fifth-year graduate students. All academic and professional fields are funded by one or more of these fellowships. These fellowships fund master's and doctoral degree programs.

General Information

Undergraduate students are often interested in pursuing study or research programs in the year following graduation. Students in this category should start looking at Fulbright, Rotary, or Marshall programs during the spring semester of their junior year. This is especially true for Rotary and Fulbright fellowships. Almost all colleges and universities have information on these programs readily accessible to interested students. The undergraduate dean's office and the career center are good places to start looking for information. The potential for getting funded in this category is good for students who have sufficient language skills and interesting study plans or research projects and who have made connections abroad.

While truly exceptional academic credentials are required for the Rhodes and Marshall, that is not necessarily the case for Rotary or Fulbright, where good language skills, good proposals, and assertiveness are just as important. Rotary, especially, takes a very organized applicant who is willing to make contact with a Rotary Club and be enthusiastic about presenting a study proposal to that group with lots of follow-up to make sure the application is endorsed.

Students in many areas of graduate study may also be interested in study or research abroad, particularly those studying languages and literature and international area studies. Anyone with qualifications to do foreign course work or conduct research abroad should actively pursue fellowship and grant opportunities because the chances of getting partial or full financial support are quite good.

Application Advice

1. *Start very early.* All arrangements to study or do research abroad take more time than you can imagine. Starting eighteen months before the desired date of departure should be sufficient. There are several reasons for starting early. The first is that many competitions, like the Fulbright, have a two-stage process in which applications are reviewed first in the United States and then in the host country. Some competitions, like Rotary, have a long process of review in the United States, where applications are considered at the local level and then go on to regional and national reviews. Some, including Rhodes and Marshall, have an interviewing process for finalists.

   Contacts abroad are usually crucial to a successful application. These can be hard to come by, especially in less developed areas, where Internet, phone, and even mail communications are not always reliable. Graduate students doing research should be especially careful to establish contacts sufficiently ahead of application deadlines. A letter from the contact confirming a place to either study or do research can be very important. Funding agencies are wary of giving money to a student who has no connections with people abroad. If, for example, access to an archive is crucial to your research, then a letter from the archive should accompany the application thus assuring access to materials. If you intend to study a certain group of people, then be sure to include a letter from an expert in the field in the country assuring that such research is possible. Collaboration with faculty or researchers abroad must be verified in writing.

If you wish to study at a foreign institution, you should already be in contact with the program or, even better, have been admitted to the institution.

2. *Become informed about the area where you wish to study or carry out research.* A surprising number of applicants know something about the country within their field but hardly anything about the society in general. Since you must live successfully within the culture, you should demonstrate that you possess prior knowledge about the historical, political, and cultural milieu.

3. *Be relevant and country-specific about what you want to do.* It is not good enough, for example, to want to study history in England. Funding agencies must be convinced that you have a compelling reason to go to the country to which you are applying. If you can get the information in the United States, why should someone pay you to travel abroad? Be sure to explain what it is that you can do in a foreign country that you cannot do at home. Analyzing the archaeological stratigraphy of Ithaka, for example, in search of protogeometric period pottery can be done only in Greece and is much more compelling than simply stating a desire to study Greek archaeology.

4. *Know your topic thoroughly.* Nothing makes a review panel happier than to see that you know the topic thoroughly. As the unexamined life to Socrates was not worth living, so the unexamined topic to a funding agency is not worth supporting. For graduate students, this means demonstrating an intimate understanding of what others in the field think about the topic through a review of the literature as well as detailing an acceptable methodology for approaching the research.

5. *Provide a reasonable timetable for accomplishing your study program or research plan.* Creating a timetable is not easy. If you have no prior experiences abroad, especially in research, it is hard to know what

is feasible. Most applicants overstate the potential outcomes and therefore sound unreasonable. Talk to someone in the field who has done related research and find out what is doable within the proposed time constraints.

6. *Have language abilities sufficient to carry out your study/research program and to live successfully within the culture.* If you do not have the skills at application time, describe how you will get those skills before the overseas period begins. Let's say you want to study ancient religious texts in Italy. You would need to demonstrate superior facility in Latin or Greek or probably both. Agencies are more flexible when training in a language or dialect is difficult to obtain, but you must offer a convincing plan for acquiring the necessary skills. Many applications fail because, although the project was carefully researched, knowledge of the topic was extraordinary, the time-frame was reasonable, and faculty support was strong, the review panel was not convinced that the applicant's language skills were up to speed.

7. *Be sure your references are one hundred percent behind the proposal.* Your references' enthusiasm for the project and the impression you will make abroad are very important. Since conditions in other countries often add impediments to successful completion of programs and projects, funding agencies are even more concerned than usual about recommendations. Be sure the recommender is appropriate to the application.

   Every doctoral student must have strong, unwavering support from his or her research director. Undergraduate and graduate students needs at least three references who will assure review panels that they are academically prepared to study or do research in another country, that they will adapt to the culture, and that they will make a good impression as Americans.

8. *Communicate the importance of making a good impression abroad.* The ambassadorial qualifications of applicants are crucial to all study or research abroad proposals. Many programs, like Fulbright, have been developed to expand good will among nations. Rotary fellowships are also very concerned about the impressions their fellows make while abroad. Your understanding of how to be a congenial American needs to be in the application materials, perhaps in a statement of personal goals and objectives.

Specific Fellowship Opportunities

All information, except the author's advice, is taken from the actual application packets, web site, award announcements, and other documents written by administrative agencies, or on the basis of calls to the individual agencies. Every effort has been made here to use the same language as that on the application or to paraphrase or summarize that language. For ease of reading, quotation marks are used only to draw special attention to important application sections.

1. British Marshall Scholarships

(Based on 2002–2003 Fellowships)

Administrative Agency: The Council of the British Embassy

Address: British Council USA
British Embassy
3100 Massachusetts Avenue, NW
Washington, DC 20008-3600
Phone: 202-488-2235; fax: 202-588-7918
Email: Marshall.scholar@britishcouncil-usa.org
Web: www.marshallscholarship.org/

Deadline and Notification: Early October for application submission; interviews for short-listed candidates in November.

Number of Awards: 40 per competition.

Other Related Fellowships: Rhodes, Fulbright, Rotary fellowships.

Average Number of Applicants: 800 per competition.

Award Amount: Average amount is £16,500 per year and includes cost of living allowance, tuition and fees, book grant, travel expenses, dependent spouse allowance.

Application Form: Online or from college or university, usually the undergraduate dean's office.

Purpose of Grant/Fellowship and Restrictions: The awards commemorate the post–World War II American Marshall Plan. The hope is to bring Americans who hold promise of leadership to the United Kingdom to understand and appreciate British values and establish bonds with British citizens. In addition, the awards seek to raise American awareness of the United Kingdom, especially among young scholars.

The scholarship is for two years of either undergraduate or graduate work leading to a British university degree at one of almost one hundred institutions in England, Northern Ireland, Scotland, and Wales. Applicants must apply within two years of getting their undergraduate degree and begin the fellowship no more than three years after completion of their bachelor degree. Business and applied studies students are especially encouraged to apply.

Length of Award: Two years. Up to three years for doctoral study at the universities of Cambridge, Edinburgh, and Oxford. Although most fields are acceptable, this grant is unlikely to support dental, medical, or veterinary science degrees. Those seeking advanced degrees in archaeology, anthropology, and earth sciences are also not encouraged to apply because no award is given for study away from the British university.

Applicant Eligibility: U.S. citizen or U.S. national, A-minus average after freshman year; attained a bachelor's degree before this scholarship begins.

Application Requirements: Application is made to a regional center that is either the applicant's permanent home address or present residence: *Mid-Atlantic:* Delaware, District of Columbia, Kentucky, Maryland, New Jersey, Pennsylvania, Virginia, West Virginia; *Mid-Western:* Illinois, Indiana, Iowa, Kansas, Michigan, Minnesota, Missouri, Nebraska, North Dakota, Ohio, South Dakota, Wisconsin; *North-Eastern:* Connecticut, Maine, Massachusetts, New Hampshire, New York, Rhode Island, Vermont; *South-Eastern:* Alabama, Florida, Georgia, Mississippi, North Carolina, South Carolina, Tennessee, Canal Zone, Puerto Rico, Virgin Islands; *South-Western:* Arkansas, Colorado, Louisiana, Oklahoma, New Mexico, Texas; *Western:* Alaska, Arizona, California, Hawaii, Idaho, Montana, Nevada, Oregon, Utah, Washington, Wyoming.

If interviewed, applicant must present evidence of birth date, citizenship, and, if applicable, marriage. Further requirements include: GRE test scores for economics; GMAT test scores for management studies; four references; all transcripts; endorsement by a high-ranking official of the applicant's college or university.

Application Comments and Advice: Most colleges and universities have a faculty advisor who will help you with the application. Be sure to seek this person out. Applicants need to find out as much as they can about British universities because a first and second choice must be indicated. In addition, a course of study and/or research must be described and knowledge of institutional programs is essential.

Those applying for doctoral programs are advised to contact British faculty and arrange a research program along with gaining admission. Links to universities can be accessed through the British Council web site.

Remember when filling out the application that the British Marshall Committee will select potential leaders who are interested in the culture of the United Kingdom. Leadership skills should be emphasized, as should a keen interest in British culture. Because numerous applicants seek admission to Oxford and Cambridge, you should investigate other university options since not all awardees go to those two institutions.

2. Deutscher Akademischer AustauschDienst Grants (DAAD)

(Based on 2002–2003 DAAD Grants)

Administrative Agency: German Academic Exchange

Address: German Academic Exchange Service
871 United Nations Plaza
New York, NY 10017
Phone: 212-758-3223; fax: 212-755-5780
Email: daadny@daad.org
Web: www.daad.org

Deadline and Notification: October submission to campus coordinator; the application must be at the German Academic Exchange Service by November 1; mid-March for award notification.

Number of Awards: 30 per competition. Note: if you combine DAAD with Fulbright, which is done in the Fulbright IIE (Institute for International Education) booklet, there are around 180 grants and fellowships for study/research in Germany.

Other Related Fellowships: Fulbright IIE, Rotary fellowships.

Average Number of Applicants: Around 470 per competition for all DAAD and German Fulbright IIE grants and fellowships.

Award Amount: 1,250–1,700 DM per month. Travel and health insurance allowances.

Application Form: From on-campus representative, usually the Fulbright officer. DAAD has arrangements with some but not all U.S. universities. Check your German department. Application is made through your university only.

Purpose of Grant/Fellowship and Restrictions: To support graduating seniors and graduate students doing study or research at German universities or institutes. Ph.D. students at the dissertation level are preferred for this grant. See Fulbright IIE grants below for more opportunities for study, research, and teaching for graduating seniors.

Length of Award: Ten months. There are also some special two-month language training grants for those who need extra language training. DAAD also offers other programs for students. Check with your DAAD and/or Fulbright IIE coordinator or in the German department.

Applicant Eligibility: U.S. or Canadian students enrolled at a DAAD partner institution. Foreign nationals may apply but first need to contact DAAD for eligibility. Preference given to students who have been invited by a German faculty member to study or do research at a particular institution. Most fields in the arts, humanities, social sciences are acceptable. Not welcome to apply are students in dentistry, medicine, pharmacy, veterinary medicine.

Applicants may not have had a DAAD for three years prior to application. For example, a student who has had a DAAD after their senior year in college would be eligible to apply again about the time he or she was doing dissertation research, as long as the research differed from the first grant.

Application Requirements: Completion of a generic DAAD application, which is submitted through the applicant's university. Passport photos, two letters of recommendation, all transcripts, evidence of contact in Germany, language evaluation. Some campus coordinators may require a simultaneous application to Fulbright IIE.

Application Comments and Advice: Previous study or research in Germany does not affect being selected for a DAAD. Key to this grant is an established contact at a German university, institute or laboratory. Start working on contacts early, during the spring and summer prior to application. Written invitations are crucial to being selected. Although email has made contacts easier, it is still important to be organized for this competition. Faculty in German departments should be very helpful in making recommendations about German institutions and German faculty contacts; the DAAD coordinator may also be helpful. On some campuses the application process is similar to that conducted for IIE Fulbrights. The process may include an on-campus interview with the Fulbright Committee.

Students in the arts should be prepared to send materials such as videos and slide portfolios along with the application.

3. Fulbright (IIE) Grants for Graduate Study, Research, and Teaching Abroad

(Based on 2002–2003 Fulbright Grants)

Administrative Agency: Institute for International Education

Address: IIE

       U.S. Student Programs Division
       809 United Nations Plaza
       New York, NY 10017-3580
       Phone: 212-984-5330; fax: 212-984-5325
       Web: www.iie.org/fulbright

Deadline: On-campus submission deadlines vary by school but are usually in September; at-large submission in October. Award notification between January and June. Note on notification: if you have not heard about an award be sure to call IIE or consult with your on-campus administrator. Our campus once had an award that was not announced until late July after the student had already gone to Costa Rica. By keeping in contact with IIE we were able to establish in May that the award was 90 percent likely to happen and we were able to keep in contact with the applicant so the award could be accepted, even at that late date.

Number of Awards: 960 for 2000–2001; 953 for 2001–2002.

Other Related Fellowships: DAAD, Marshall, Rhodes, NSEP fellowships.

Average Number of Applicants: Over 4,000 per competition.

Award Amount: Varies according to country. The award usually includes transportation; tuition, books, and research allowance; and room and board supplement.

Application Form: Applications for the on-campus competition can be obtained through the Fulbright officer; at-large applicants (those not applying through a college or university campus but directly to IIE) should contact IIE through their web site or by phone or mail.

Purpose of Grant/Fellowship and Restrictions: The purpose of the award is to promote better relations with other nations. Recent college graduates, graduate students at all levels, artists, and young professionals in most fields may study, do research, or teach abroad. Each country establishes what type of study, research, and teaching is available. Teaching is limited to these countries: Belgium/Luxembourg: teaching English conversation in universities; France: teaching English conversation in secondary schools and teacher-training institutions; Germany: teaching English, American studies, and literature in high schools; Hungary: teaching English in selected institutions; Korea: teaching English in middle schools; Turkey: two positions are available for teaching American literature and/or English.

Length of Award: Usually a year, with a one-year renewal possible.

Applicant Eligibility: U.S. citizen; completion of a bachelor's degree prior to grant implementation; sufficient language skills; good health. Preference is given to applicants who have not studied or resided in the country applied to for more that six months, although junior year or study abroad will not disqualify an applicant. All factors being equal, veterans receive preference.

M.D.s must have that degree at time of application. Applicants may hold a J.D. Applicants to Germany under DAAD program may hold a Ph.D. Applicants applying for postdoctoral research in Israel must have completed the Ph.D.

Application Requirements: Completed application; official transcripts; language evaluation; creative and performing artists should include samples of work. At-large applicants apply through IIE. At-large or other candidates may attend preparation workshops orchestrated by IIE and usually held five times a year in New York City, Chicago, Denver, Houston, San Francisco, and Washington, D.C. At-large applicants are urged to attend one of these workshops or a preparation session held on a college campus. On-campus applicants must work with a campus Fulbright officer. Recent graduates not currently enrolled may utilize their undergraduate institutional system for help in applying. The on-campus procedure usually includes preparation workshops, all materials needed for the application, help with country and project identification, and on-campus interview with a faculty committee.

Each country has specific requirements; for example, Albania wants one mature graduate student in the field of history and/or linguistics who has no dependents. Most countries are not that restrictive, but getting the IIE booklet early on is important in understanding country interests.

Application Comments and Advice: The application process is complicated, so start very early, at least eighteen months before you want to go abroad. Early contact with the Fulbright officer in the spring, some six months before the application deadline, is basic. Contacts with institutions overseas should be made prior to application. Letters from contacts willing to assist in research or an admission to an academic program carry a lot of weight in the selection process.

Applicants are judged on how much the project will promote good will among nations; how well the project matches the country's interest; and the ratio of applications to available positions. Important to the proposal is a justification of why the study/research project must be done in the chosen country. You must have given proven consideration to choosing the country and provide specific reasons why what is proposed cannot be done elsewhere. Maybe vital papers are located only in a certain archives in Budapest, for example. Reasons must be carefully spelled out. Remember to emphasize the idea of mutual understanding between the United States and the country when appropriate.

Consult with faculty and committee members to construct a reasonable time frame for completion of your project. Most people overestimate what can be done in a year. Contacts abroad can be helpful in this area.

Be sure your language skills are up to speed before you apply. In cases of unusual languages where training is hard to obtain, have a plan for getting the proper skills prior to departure or, in some unusual cases, upon arrival abroad.

The application packet gives a sense of what kinds of candidates the interviewers and IIE seek. Read it carefully. When you are interviewed, be ready to demonstrate your knowledge about the culture, politics, and history of the country to which you are applying.

Fulbright is looking for people who are genuinely interested in and who care about citizens of other cultures. It also seeks fellows who have good ambassadorial skills and who will represent the United States in a positive way. Be sure to reflect these qualities in your statement.

4. Fulbright-Hays Doctoral Dissertation Research Abroad Program

(Based on 2002–2003 Fellowships)
Administrative Agency: U.S. Department of Education
Address: U.S. Department of Education
      Higher Education Programs
      1990 K Street, NW
      Washington, DC 20006-8521
      Phone: 202-502-7700
      Email: OPE_IEGPS@ed.gov
      Web: www.ed.gov/offices/OPE/HEP/iegps/ddrap.html
Deadline and Notification: Late October for applications submission; late March to early April for award notification. Award notification is done through the applicant's institution.
Number of Awards: 115 fellowships in 2001.
Other Related Fellowships: Fulbright, NSEP, IREX fellowships.
Average Number of Applicants: 417 in 2000.
Award Amount: Each country is different. A chart lists the amounts per country. Award includes travel expenses, maintenance, and dependents allowances; project expenses like books and affiliation fees; health and accident insurance.
Application Form: Online at above web site.
Purpose of Grant/Fellowship and Restrictions: To fund dissertation research in modern foreign languages and area studies in non-Western countries. Areas funded in 2000 (with number of awards in parentheses) were Africa (15), Western Hemisphere (15), Central/Eastern Europe/ Eurasia (14), East Asia (13), Near East (12), South Asia (10), and Southeast Asia (9). Disciplines supported in 2000 include: anthropology, archeology, architecture, biology, economics, ethnomusicology, comparative literature, ecology, folklore, geography, history, languages and literatures, political science, and sociology.
Length of Award: Six months to one year.
Applicant Eligibility: Students must apply through their university. Although application may be retrieved online, it must be processed through the institution. U.S. citizen, U.S. national, permanent resident; graduate students who are candidates for doctoral degrees, are planning a teaching career in the United States, and have adequate language skills to conduct research.

Application Requirements: Completed application, including numerous forms which must be filled out by the university; three recommendations; language evaluation; good health. The application and instructions are more than fifty pages, but much of it is institutional paperwork.

Application Comments and Advice: The application includes a sample of the evaluation form used for grading the quality of the project (60 points) and the applicant's qualifications (40 points). The two areas are broken down into subratings. For example, under the quality of the project area are sections like "the major hypothesis" (10 points) and "justification for overseas research" (10 points). The rating form should become your guide to structuring the description of the research project, because it will be used for evaluation. The more closely you follow the rating form, the better your score will be. If a reviewer has to hunt for appropriate responses, he or she may get frustrated and conclude that you are disorganized. As a result, you will lose points.

The 40 points assigned to qualifications includes a review of the overall academic record, academic record in the area of the proposed project, language proficiency, and success in previous overseas experiences. The Department of Education is enthusiastic about applicants who have had overseas experience, the more the better. Information for this section will be gotten from letters of reference, course work and grades, and your curriculum vitae (resume).

Letters of reference must be unfailingly supportive, especially from your dissertation advisor. It is important that the referees communicate that you can work well abroad.

The curriculum vitae information should be related to your research and course of study. For example, this is a good place to explain any prior experiences abroad.

Be sure to have a physician or nurse practitioner certify your physical and psychological ability to carry out the project. Failure to do so will jeopardize the application.

This application takes a lot of running around to advisors, dean's offices, research offices, and so on. You must be willing to follow up to make sure everyone who needs to sign off has done so and that every form that needs to be filled out has been completed. It is helpful to have a dean or faculty advocate who is willing to act on your behalf if someone else at the university drops the ball.

If you need an evaluation in a less commonly taught language, the Department of Education will find an evaluator if you cannot.

Be sure to include letters from contacts abroad who can assure you have access to whatever you need to do your project. That means you must start early because contacts in many countries are difficult to obtain and the evidence must be in writing.

If you are rejected, try to find out why and apply again. The agency expects and encourages reapplication.

You are responsible for your own visas, passports, and research clearances. Several years ago a Palestinian student who was a permanent resident of the U.S. won an award to study in Turkey. He had no passport and had a terrible time getting permission to travel. A month of almost daily phone calls to the Department of Education, the Department of State, and so on eventually solved the problem. The point is you really need to follow this process. The Department of Education will really try hard to solve any hurdles that pop up along the way.

5. International Research and Exchange Board (IREX) Grants for Central and Eastern Europe, Eurasia, Mongolia, Turkey, and Iran

(Based on 2002–2003 IREX Grants)

Administrative Agency: IREX

Address: IREX
2121 K Street, NW, Suite 700
Washington, DC 20037
Phone: 202-628-8188; fax: 202-628-8189
Email: irex@irex.org
Web: www.irex.org

Deadline: Deadlines vary according to program. See below.

Number of Awards: Number of awards varies according to program. See below. Awards usually include round-trip airfare and visa fees and a stipend for living expenses including room and board.

Other Related Fellowships: Fulbright, especially Fulbright-Hays, NSEP fellowships.

Average Number of Applicants: Varies by program.

Award Amount: Varies by program.

Application Form: Online or from the above address.

Purpose of Grant/Fellowship and Restrictions: IREX fosters research in Central and Eastern Europe, Eurasia, Mongolia, Turkey, and Iran. In addition, IREX awardees become part of an ongoing network. IREX will publish alumni research abstracts and short papers; place alumni names in a directory of experts; invite alumni to policy forums, receptions, conferences; provide an electronic mailing list and IREX publications.

IREX alumni are invited to serve on the award selection committees; host visiting scholars; present at policy forums. IREX offers numerous research opportunities which are funded by a variety of sources including the National Endowment for the Humanities and the U.S. Department of State. Two are most suited to graduate students: IREX Individual Advanced Research Opportunities and IREX Mongolia Research Fellowship Program.

General Applicant Eligibility: U.S. citizen for three years prior to application. Sufficient language ability. For Individual Advanced Research grant, full-time affiliation with college or university as faculty member or Ph.D. student at the dissertation stage, as well as independent scholars.

IREX Individual Advanced Research Opportunities

For research in the *Central and Eastern European countries* of: Albania, Bosnia and Herzegovina, Bulgaria, Croatia, Czech Republic, Estonia, Federal Republic of Yugoslavia, Hungary, Iran, Latvia, Lithuania, Macedonia, Poland, Romania, Slovakia, Slovenia, and Turkey.

For research in the *Eurasian countries* of: Armenia, Azerbaijan, Belarus, Georgia, Iran, Kazakhstan, Kirghizstan, Moldova, Russian Federation, Tadzhikistan, Turkey, Turkmenistan, Ukraine, and Uzbekistan.

Awards and Deadline: 37 awards. November submission deadline. Applications must be received by the deadline date. Everything, including letters of reference must be at IREX by the deadline. March award notification.

Applicants are encouraged to apply for a Fulbright-Hays simultaneously.

Fields of research include: all fields but especially social sciences, business, economics, international relations, comparative and interdisciplinary studies. The research should contribute to the knowledge base of the area especially in the realm of U.S. foreign policy.

The 1,600-word proposal should include reasons for going abroad, an outline of specific activities to be undertaken, a list of any sites such as archives that will be utilized, the feasibility of completing the research, and problems that might arise. Any contacts that make the research feasible should be listed in the proposal and letters from contacts should be included.

Grants are for two to nine months for predoctoral and postdoctoral research. Permanent residents may apply.

IREX Mongolia Research Fellowship Program

Program not offered in 2002; may be offered in 2003.

Fields acceptable for research include most social sciences; business; applied and fine arts; music and musicology; architecture; international relations; literature; military science; communications;

journalism; library science; theatre; criminology; law; religion, and others. Applicant must have completed doctoral degree or be Ph.D. candidate.

Number of Awards and Deadline: 7 or 8 awards. Late January submission deadline.

The web site offers excellent information about travel, research institutions, culture, history, and politics in Mongolia.

In addition to the research awards, IREX also offers four fellowships in Mongolian Language Training. Nine weeks of language immersion in Ulaanbaator is provided. The award is available to undergraduates, graduate students, and postdoctoral researchers. The language training is tentatively scheduled for summer. The deadline is early December.

6. Japanese Government Monbusho Scholarships for Language and Culture Study and for Research

(Based on 2002 Scholarships)

Administrative Agency: Consulate General of Japan

Address: This grant is available through all the Japanese consulates in the United States. Consulates are located in the following cities: Atlanta: www.cgj-hagatna.org/; Anchorage: www.embjapan/anchorage/; Boston: www.embjapan/boston/; Chicago: www.embjapan/chicago/; Denver: www.embjapan/denver/; Detroit: www.embjapan/detroit/; Honolulu: www.embjapan/honolulu/; Kansas City: www.embjapan/kansascity/; Los Angeles: www.embjapan/la/; New Orleans: www.embjapan/neworleans/; New York: //ny.cgj.org/index.html; Portland, OR: www.embjapan/portland/; San Francisco: www.embjapan/sf/; Seattle: www. embjapan/seattle/. Contact the nearest office or:

> Embassy of Japan
> 2520 Massachusetts Avenue, NW
> Washington, DC 20008
> Phone: 202-238-6700; fax: 202-338-2187
> Web: www.embjapan.org

Monbusho Language and Japanese Culture Scholarships

Deadline: Mid-April for application submission; about a week later for language examination and interview; grant to begin in October. (Each embassy or consulate may have a slightly different schedule.)

Other Related Fellowships: NSEP scholarships.

Award Amount: 142,500 yen per month; travel and field study allowances; tuition and fees; partial health coverage.

Application Form: Locate the nearest Japanese consulate or contact the embassy at the address above.

Purpose of Grant/Fellowship and Restrictions: To encourage college students and college graduates to further their language skills and cultural studies knowledge through course work in Japan.

Length of Award: One academic year.

Applicant Eligibility: U.S. citizens, 18–29 years old, with prior course work in Japanese language.

Application Requirements: A completed application.

Monbusho Scholarships for Research

Deadline: September for application submission; language exam and interview a week or so later.

Number of Awards: 40 per competition.

Other Related Fellowships: Fulbright, Fulbright-Hays, NSEP fellowships.

Average Number of Applicants: The number can vary according to the specific consulate, which do not seem to be in contact with each other regarding scholarships.

Award Amount: 185,000 yen per month. Travel; field study allowance; waiver of tuition and fees; partial health insurance.

Application Form: From nearest embassy or consulate. Application must be made to nearest consulate.

Purpose of Grant/Fellowship and Restrictions: To provide research opportunities to American students in all fields. Researchers will be assigned to a university as a non-degree affiliate.

Length of Award: Eighteen months to two years.

Applicant Eligibility: U.S. citizen; 34 years old or under; sufficient language skills to carry out research.

Acceptable fields of study: *Humanities and Social Sciences:* literature, history, aesthetics, law, politics, economics, commerce, pedagogy, psychology, sociology, music, fine arts, and others. *Natural Sciences:* pure science, engineering, agriculture, fisheries, pharmacology, medicine, dentistry, home economics.

Application Requirements: A completed application submitted to nearest consulate. Getting a current application may take some doing, depending upon the consulate.

Application Comments and Advice: The quality of the proposed plan of research, the level of language skills, and the interview are the primary criteria for selection. Be sure to provide a time line for research that is feasible. Your reasons for going to Japan to do research must be compelling. You also need to be persistent in getting information from the embassy or consulate.

7. National Security Education Program David L. Boren Graduate Fellowships for Language and Area Studies (NSEP)

(Based on 2002–2003 Fellowship)
Administrative Agency: Academy for Educational Development
Address: Academy for Educational Development
        1825 Connecticut Avenue, NW
        Washington, DC 20009-5721
        Phone: 800-498-9360 *or* 202-884-8285; fax: 202-884-8407
        Email: nsep@aed.org
        Web: www.aed.org/nsep
Deadline and Notification: Mid-January for application submission; late April for award notification.
Number of Awards: 90–100 per competition.
Award Information: See Chapter 3 for complete information.
Purpose of Grant/Fellowship and Restrictions: This scholarship has a one-year overseas component for language training and research in eighty countries in forty-five languages. Not supported are language training and research related to Western Europe, Canada, Australia, or New Zealand. NSEP supports study and research that relate to the national security of the United States as well as sustainable development, environmental degradation, global disease and hunger, population growth and migration, and economic competitiveness. Most fields are acceptable. Within five years of award completion, awardees must begin a job in a federal or independent agency or office specified in the grant information. Academic service may be substituted if no job can be found in above areas.

8. Rhodes Scholarships for Study at Oxford University

(Based on 2002–2003 Rhodes Scholarship)
Administrative Agency: Rhodes Scholarship Trust
Address: Rhodes Scholarship Trust
        Office of the American Secretary
        8229 Boone Boulevard, Suite 240
        Vienna, VA 22182
        Email: amsec@rhodesscholar.org
        Web: www.rhodesscholar.org. *Note:* The Rhodes administration rotates and the address can change. The web site is the most reliable address.
Deadline: Mid-October for submission.
Number of Awards: 32 per competition.

Other Related Fellowships: Marshall, Fulbright, Rotary fellowships.

Award Amount: At least £735 per month, plus tuition and fees.

Application Form: Online, through the mail, or from office on campus.

Purpose of Grant/Fellowship and Restrictions: To bring talented American students to Oxford University to study for a second undergraduate or first graduate degree. Master's degrees are the most popular. All fields are acceptable. The Rhodes committees are looking for students who will become leaders in their field and are especially attracted to applicants who will participate in activities beyond those academic, particularly something of a physical nature. Lots of energy is important.

Length of Award: Two years with a possible third for doctoral study.

Applicant Eligibility: U.S. citizen at time of application. Rhodes also offers this fellowship to citizens of other countries as well. Canadians are offered eleven fellowships a year, Australians and South Africans nine each, Indians six, Germans four, and so on. Check the web site if you are not an American citizen to see if your country is part of the program.

Applicants must be eighteen to twenty-four years old and have a bachelor's degree before award begins. Most applicants are seniors in college. Applicants may be married, but no spousal support is offered and the literature says non-British spouses will find it very hard to find work in Britain.

Application Requirements: A completed application which includes your college's endorsement, academic transcripts, copy of birth certificate, and five to eight letters of recommendation, four of which must be from faculty who are familiar with the applicant's academic record. The rest may be character references related to community service and other qualities.

The Rhodes committees advise getting at least five academic references because failure to supply four will result in disqualification. Since letters can be slow in coming, it is best to hedge your bets with at least one extra.

If your campus has a Rhodes facilitator, that would be the best help available. There is a list of campus advisors on the Rhodes web site, although I found it to be out of date in mid-2001.

The process is complicated, especially the institutional endorsement requirement and the large number of recommendations. Start early. The new application is available online in the summer.

Application is made to a state secretary. You will have to figure out which is the most appropriate state to use as residency. The web site gives a list of ways to sort this out. Since these state secretaries are bound to change from time to time, be sure to have the most current application packet. The state secretaries are usually faculty members and/or Rhodes alumni.

The applications are reviewed at the state level and those deemed the best are then sent to one of the eight regional districts for further consideration. At each level selected students are interviewed. (Rhodes pays travel expenses to the district committee interview but not to the state interview.) Four awardees are selected from each of the eight districts.

Application Comments and Advice: Persistence is important. Over and over again the literature emphasizes four standards by which the applicants will be judged. (1) Literary and scholastic achievements. (2) Energy to use one's talents to the full, as exemplified by fondness for and success in sports (sports once meant varsity-level accomplishments but that is no longer the case; check the Q & A section on the web site for more information). (3) Truth, courage, devotion to duty, sympathy for and protection of the weak, kindliness, unselfishness, and fellowship. (4) Moral force of character and instincts to lead, and to take an interest in one's fellow beings. Be sure to give a list of these standards to your recommenders as a guide. Also give them a list of all your grades, honors, achievements, and interests (both athletic and non-athletic) and any volunteer work done so they can use specific examples of how you meet the standards above. Also remember to address these standards in your application statements.

You should study the opportunities at Oxford and be knowledgeable about the program to which you aspire. The Q & A section states that the committees "look for sincere desire to study there (Committees try hard to screen out those sharp-elbowed applicants interested in the great honor only, and not in applying themselves at Oxford)." The point is that the Rhodes committees are looking for humble but talented students who are most interested in the welfare of others and who will approach their studies and their outside activities with a high level of energy and commitment. Study the list of former recipients on the web site to get a feel for the type of person Rhodes seeks.

9. Rotary Academic Year, Multi-Year, and Cultural Ambassadorial Scholarships

(Based on 2003–2004 Rotary Scholarships)
Administrative Agency: Rotary Foundation of Rotary International
Address: The Rotary Foundation
   One Rotary Center
   1560 Sherman Avenue
   Evanston, IL 60201-3698
   Phone: 847-866-3000; fax: 847-328-8554

Email: scholarshipinquiries@rotary.org
Web: www.rotary.org

Deadline and Notification: Deadlines vary according to local Rotary Club but are between March and June one year before the award begins. To go abroad in August 2005, for example, you need to apply in the spring of 2004. Notification of award in December of the application year.

Rotary Academic Year Scholarships

Number of Awards: One thousand fellowships are offered worldwide per competition. Around 336 are available to U.S. citizens. More than sixty nations sponsor scholarships each year.

Other Related Fellowships: British Marshall, DAAD, Fulbright, Rhodes fellowships.

Award Amount: $13,000–$25,000 depending on the country and institution.

Application Form: Online or from the above address.

Purpose of Grant/Fellowship and Restrictions: To foster goodwill between sponsoring and host countries. The scholars chosen should contribute to international understanding through their research and study. Applicants should be flexible regarding assigned areas and institutions.

Length of Award: One academic year.

Applicant Eligibility: Applicant must be a citizen of a country that has established Rotary clubs. Two years of college-level work completed. No Rotarians or children or grandchildren of Rotarians may apply. Disabled persons are encouraged to apply. Language proficiency required.

Application Requirements: Completed application submitted to a Rotary Club. All transcripts, language ability form, two recommendations, five choices of countries and institutions. Applicants must be willing to give ten to fifteen talks to Rotary and non-Rotary groups during the scholarship period. Also, awardees are expected to learn about and promote Rotary whenever possible and be willing to participate in Rotary public relations events.

Application Comments and Advice: The application starts out at the local level and proceeds to district then national levels. Persistence is important in applying for a Rotary. Since every club has its own competition rules, candidates must be willing to seek out information and nudge local Rotarians into endorsing their application.

You might have to go to a Rotary Club lunch and explain why study abroad is so important and how good an ambassador you will be. The ability to speak publicly and the willingness to do so are crucial.

It is most important to start early. The application deadline is much earlier than most scholarships and getting a club endorsement may take awhile.

If you find anyone who has won the scholarship you should get their advice on this fellowship more than almost any other.

Rotary Multi-Year Scholarships are for two years of full-time degree study in almost any field. Flat grant of around $12,000 a year. The application procedures and advice are the same as above.

Rotary Cultural Ambassadorial Scholarships are for three to six months of intensive language training and cultural immersion. The award is for up to $19,000 but most awardees receive a lot less. The application procedures and advice are the same as above. Languages available for training include: Arabic, French, German, Hebrew, Japanese, Italian, Korean, Mandarin Chinese, Polish, Portuguese, Russian, Spanish, Swahili, and Swedish.

10. Social Science Research Council (SRRC) International Predissertation Fellowships; Fellowships for the Study of the Russian Empire, the Soviet Union, and Its Successor States; and Predissertation Fellowships for Bangladesh

(Based on 2002–2003 Fellowships)
Administrative Agency: Social Science Research Council
Address: Social Science Research Council
         810 Seventh Avenue
         New York, NY 10019
         Phone: 212-377-2700; fax: 212-377-2727
         Email: International: ipfp@ssrc.org; Russian: eurasia@ssrc.org;
         Bangladesh: s-asia@ssrc.org; general: info@ssrc.org
         Web: www.ssrc.org

SSRC International Predissertation Fellowship
Deadline: August or September, depending on the university.
Number of Awards: 21 per competition.
Other Related Fellowships: Fulbright, Rotary, NSEP fellowships.
Award Amount: Amount depends on geographic area of study.
Application Form: From the participating universities: University of California, Berkeley, UCLA, University of California, San Diego, University of Chicago, Columbia, Cornell, Duke, Harvard, University of Illinois (Urbana), Indiana University (Bloomington), MIT, Michigan State, University of Michigan (Ann Arbor), University of Minnesota

(Twin Cities), University of North Carolina (Chapel Hill), North-western, University of Pennsylvania, Princeton, Stanford, University of Texas (Austin), University of Washington, University of Wisconsin (Madison), Yale.

Purpose of Grant/Fellowship and Restrictions: To support social science students interested in careers in research and teaching in the pursuit of topics related to the developing world. Of special interest are those applicants "who appreciate the extent to which contemporary issues are rooted in the histories and culture of specific places"; and, "whose scholarship is firmly grounded in the methodologies and analytic approaches." The program especially seeks students in economics, political science, psychology, and sociology, but is open to other disciplines in the social sciences. The aim is to facilitate field research for dissertation preparation in the following areas: Africa, Central Asia and the Caucasus, China, Latin America and the Caribbean, the Near and Middle East, South Asia and Southeast Asia.

Two types of fellowship are available:

Standard Fellowship: Twelve months of support over two years for language training, overseas study, and course work.

Advanced Disciplinary Training Fellowship: Twelve months over two years of U.S. coursework in disciplinary theory and method. Applicant must work with an advisor to develop a twelve-month plan to be submitted to SSRC. This is for students with especially strong backgrounds in area studies.

Length of Award: Twelve months.

Applicant Eligibility: Enrollment in a doctoral program at one of the above listed universities.

Application Requirements: A completed application.

Application Comments and Advice: See below a summary of advice for all SRRS fellowships.

SSRC Fellowships for Study of the Russian Empire, the Soviet Union and Its Successor States for Graduate Training; Dissertation Write-Up; Postdoctoral Employment and Tenure Opportunity Improvement

Purpose: The U.S. Department of State offers three types of SSRC fellowships

   (a) Graduate Training: $10,000 for three to nine months to enable students to strengthen their area studies knowledge in language and culture and to undertake an exploratory trip abroad for dissertation planning.

   (b) Dissertation Write-up: $15,000 for one academic year to finish the dissertation.

(c) Postdoctoral: $24,000 to help improve employment and tenure opportunities of recent Ph.D. recipients. Covers living, travel, and research costs and can be spread over two years. The preferred pattern is two summers and one semester of sabbatical.

Research in the non-Russian regions and states of the former Soviet Union is of special interest.

Deadline: November 1.

Eligibility: U.S. citizens or permanent residents. For (a) and (b), enrollment in a doctoral program in the humanities or social sciences. For (c), must have received a Ph.D. within six years in humanities or social sciences.

Number of Awards: Fourteen for training, dissertation write-up, and postdoctoral combined.

Application Advice and Comment: See below for advice for all SSRC fellowships.

SSRC Bangladesh Predissertation Fellowships

Purpose: Ford Foundation supports research for travel and research in Bangladesh.

Award: $5,200 for three to four months of field research for seeking research sites and materials, language skills improvement, and establishment of contacts.

Deadline: December 1.

Number of Awards: Up to 4 per competition.

Eligibility: Completion of at least one year of study leading to a Ph.D. in social sciences or humanities at a North American university. No citizenship requirements.

SSCR Application Writing Advice

The web site provides a very good "Art of Writing Proposals" section by Adam Przeworski of New York University and Frank Salomon of the University of Wisconsin. The topics—which include Capture the Reviewer's Attention, Aim for Clarity, Establish the Context, What's the Payoff, Use a Fresh Approach, Describe Your Methodology, Specify Your Objectives—can be very helpful in writing your proposal. They give insights into how the SSRC reviews applications, so be sure to give this section a very careful reading.

Chapter 5
Research Grants

This chapter presents general information and application writing advice for research grants for which an individual may apply. It also describes in detail certain specific grant opportunities, namely:

1. American Museum of Natural History Research Grants
2. Explorers Club Exploration Fund Grants
3. Geological Society of America Grants for Support of Graduate Student Research
4. Charles A. and Anne Morrow Lindbergh Grants for Research in Technology and the Preservation of the Natural/Human Environment
5. Phillips Fund Grants for Native American Studies
6. White House and Presidential Library Travel and Research Grants
7. Sigma Xi Research Grants
8. Social Science Research Council (SSRC) Fellowships in Applied Economics.

Grants listed in this section are of interest to junior and senior undergraduates, first- through fifth-year graduate students, and postdocs. Fields funded by one or more of these grants are the social sciences, humanities, and engineering.

General Information

The purpose of research grants is to support work on a specific project. The project may be in the exploratory, middle, or advanced stages. Research grants are available to purchase equipment and other supplies; to conduct surveys or experiments; to provide living support; to encourage travel to collections.

Research grants are available to people at all levels including undergraduate, master's, and doctoral students in all fields.

Locating research money often takes careful detective work. While well-known opportunities are on the Internet and in publications, far more can be found through determined hunting. Reading the journals in your discipline and contacting the associations and societies within your field of study are good ways to tap these funds.

Another place to look for research money is in nonacademic, not-for-profit agencies. *The Encyclopedia of Associations,* which can be found in any large library, lists most not-for-profits of any size and is a good source of funding information.

Other sources of funds included local, state, or regional agencies and foundations that are too small to be noticed by larger databases and grant lists. Somewhere, in every state, is an organization that gathers information about these resources and makes them available either online or at a small library. State or city libraries or the Secretary of State's office can usually direct you to these sources.

State governments can also supply resources for research grant support. Many states publish a booklet describing what they fund. Sometimes it may take a series of internet searches or phone calls to various state agencies to find grant sources. Start with the Secretary of State's office. State money is typically earmarked for research in conservation, historic preservation, education, environmental improvement, social welfare, public policy, and agriculture, as well as other areas.

Museums, archives, and libraries are other sources of unadvertised research money. Because organizations are eager to have qualified scholars utilize their resources, they often set aside money for the purpose of bringing people in to study their collections, manuscripts, documents, or books. When looking for this sort of support, first determine where data is located then contact the institution either by phone or through the web site to see if grants are available.

The more famous museum library research grants may be well known, but there are many more that are not easily found and take determination and perseverance to locate.

Application Advice

1. *Hunt in out-of-the-way places.* Trade publications, journals, newsletters, career libraries on campus, specialty libraries.
2. *When a grant opportunity seems to fit your project but the organization's information is not clear, call the agency.* Email can work but I have found that you get more instant results from a phone call. Sometimes email is not answered for weeks and sometimes by a person who knows little.
3. *If the application asks for a general description of the research project be sure to indicate* the problem to be solved (or question to be answered), how the problem is to be solved (or the question answered), how

your research plan will be enhanced by the grant, what significance your research will be to the field, and who is likely to benefit from your research.

For example, say you are researching Truman's involvement in the development of the atomic bomb. You need information from the Truman library. You need to state the specifics of your research, and why you need to travel to the library and what records you want to look at and why. This would require preliminary research about what records the library has that would shed light on your project. The more specific your needs, the more likely you are to be funded.

4. *Be sure to frame the project within the context of the larger picture.* This is especially true when you are hunting for funding for part of the research.

5. *Carefully research your financial needs and prepare a realistic budget.* Consult with faculty or research office personnel for help in this area, especially if the application requirements are too complicated.

6. *Sometimes money is available only through faculty or institutional sponsorship.* If this is the case, try to find a faculty mentor who will agree to act as principal investigator.

7. *If a faculty PI is used, the project will usually go to the institution's sponsored projects office.* That means all kinds of signatures may be needed, and the budget will be reviewed outside the department. All this takes time, so start early.

Specific Grant Opportunities

The research grant opportunities listed in this section are just a sample of what is available. Be sure to consult Chapter 6, Dissertation Grants, for more details. All information, except the author's advice, is taken from the actual application information including web sites when available. Every effort is made to use the same language as that on the application or to paraphrase or summarize that language. For ease of reading, quotations marks are used only to draw attention to important application sections.

1. American Museum of Natural History Research Grants

(Based on 2002–2003 Grants)
Administrative Agency: American Museum of Natural History
Address: American Museum of Natural History
Central Park West at 79th Street

New York, NY 10024-5192
Phone: 212-769-5400; fax: 212-769-5495
Email: grants@amnh.org
Web: http://research.amnh.org

Comment: Research awards are available to advanced graduate students and postdoctoral researchers in zoology, paleontology, anthropology, astrophysics, earth and planetary sciences. The funds that house these grants are:

Frank M. Chapman Memorial Grants: for ornithology.

Lerner-Grey Grants: for marine zoology research.

Theodore Roosevelt Memorial Grants: for research in wildlife conservation other than ornithology.

Collection Study Grants: for travel and subsistence while visiting the museum collections.

Graduate Student Fellowship Program: for graduate students at specified universities in specific fields.

Deadlines and Notification:

Chapman: January 15 for submission; notification in April.

Lerner-Grey: March 15 for submission; notification in May.

Theodore Roosevelt: February 15 for submission; notification in April.

Collection Study Grants: two months prior to the intended date of visit to the museum.

Graduate Student Fellowship Program: January 31 for submission.

Number of Awards: 200 per competition.

Average Number of Applicants: 400 per competition.

Application Form: Online or from the above address.

Purpose of Grant/Fellowship and Restrictions:

Chapman: research in ornithology, neontology, and paleontology.

Lerner-Grey: marine zoology in the areas of systematics, evolution, ecology, and field-oriented behavioral studies of marine animals. No awards in botany or biochemistry.

Theodore Roosevelt: wildlife conservation or natural history related to interests of the museum.

Collection Study Grants: to travel to the museum and study the collections. Available to the following fields: anthropology, astrophysics, earth and planetary sciences, entomology, herpetology, ichthyology, mammalogy, ornithology, vertebrate paleontology.

Graduate Student Fellowships are available to students at the following universities only and in the following fields. Columbia University: anthropology, vertebrate and invertebrate paleontology, earth and planetary sciences, astrophysics, evolutionary biology. Cornell University: entomology. CUNY: evolutionary biology, systematics, biological anthropology. Yale University: molecular biology, systematics. Check with these programs for more details.

Applicant Eligibility: See each grant above.

Application Requirements: For all but Graduate Student Fellowships: A completed application which includes: a project description not longer than two pages; budget; two letters of recommendation.

Award Amount: $200–$2,000; average of $1,400 for all except the Graduate Student Fellowship.

Application Comments and Advice: Collection Study Grant applicants should first contact the museum and talk to a staff member to assess the collection relative to the proposed research. This is an application requirement. In addition, you should provide the museum with the name of a museum person with whom you will work.

Although the Chapman, Roosevelt, and Lerner-Grey grants do not require contacting the museum, common sense would indicate doing the same for these applications as for the Collection Study Grant.

With all of the above, provide a brief but detailed description of the project that includes the big as well as the little picture, the research plan including time frame, the significance of the research, the contribution it will make to science, and, importantly, the relevance to museum activities and interests.

2. Explorers Club Exploration Fund Grants

(Based on 2002 Grants)

Administrative Agency: The Explorers Club

Address: The Explorers Club
46 East 70th Street
New York, NY 10021
Phone: 212-628-8383; Fax: 212-288-4449
Email: office@explorers.org
Web: www.explorers.org

Deadline and Notification: late January for application submission; April for award announcement.

Number of Awards: 33–35 per competition.

Average Number of Applicants: 400 per competition.

Award Amount: Up to $1,200.

Application Form: Online or from the above address.

Purpose of Grant/Fellowship and Restrictions: To support primarily graduate students in exploration, field research, and expedition participation "to broaden our knowledge of the universe." Students at any stage of a master's or doctoral degree program are eligible to apply. Students in fields of anthropology, archaeology, biology, and the environmental sciences are the most likely to receive awards, although there is no articulated field restriction.

In addition to the graduate student awards, the Explorers Club has a youth activities program that funds approximately sixty high school and college students to pursue activities similar to those described above.

Length of Award: Depends upon the project. The amount usually covers transportation costs and some living expenses for a short period of time.

Applicant Eligibility: The grant is usually given to graduate students but no other eligibility requirements are listed.

Application Requirements: A completed application which is brief and requires a fifty-word statement about the research and expedition objectives (a one-page description of the expedition itself may be attached). Also required are the names and address of three people connected to the expedition who might be contacted, along with a budget.

Application Comments and Advice: The application is simple and straight-forward. Proposals are judged on their scientific and practical merits. In other words, the project must be scientifically sound and feasible. References should be willing to address these issues.

It is most important to secure a place on an expedition such as an archaeological dig or other organized research project before applying for support. It is even better if the expedition is run by or has members of the Explorers Club as participants. The principals of the project should be given as references. The Club tends toward disorganization so persistence is important. If April comes and goes and no word has been forthcoming, call to see if the awards have been made. The actual money may take a while in arriving after an award has been made. When my son was funded by the Club to dig in Greece, his check came several months after he returned from the expedition. All that said, the Club is a wonderful source of small grants for worthy projects.

3. Geological Society of America (GSA) Grants for Support of Graduate Student Research

(Based on 2002–2003 Grants)
Administrative Agency: Geological Society of America
Address: GSA
    3300 Penrose Place
    Box 9140
    Boulder, CO 80301-9140

Phone: 303-447-2020 or 800-472-1988; fax: 303-357-1070
Email: lcarter@geosociety.org
Web: www.geosociety.org

Deadline and Notification: February 1 for application submission; award notification in April.

Number of Awards: 245 per competition.

Average Number of Applicants: 600 per competition.

Award Amount: Up to $3,175 with an average of $1,622.

Application Form: Online, or from the above postal or email addresses.

Purpose of Grant/Fellowship and Restrictions: The Society aims to support master's and doctoral students in the United States, Canada, Mexico, and Central America. The awards are in geosciences and are administered by the following divisions within GSA: General Geosciences (geophysics, hydrology, sedimentary geology, structural geology, tectonics); Archaeological Geology (earth sciences and archaeology); Coal Geology; Planetary Geology; Quaternary Geology and Geomorphology; Engineering Geology; other fields of interest include paleontology, igneous and metamorphic petrology (including volcanology), and economic geology.

Length of Award: One year.

Applicant Eligibility: GSA membership.

Application Requirements: A completed application and two legible copies. No handwritten or emailed applications accepted. Two faculty recommendations.

Application Comments and Advice: Included with the application is a terrific memo entitled "A Few Suggestions for Preparation of Your Research Grant Application." Just as important is a copy of the Reviewer's Evaluation Checklist. Read both of these carefully and refer to them as you are preparing the application. From these two important documents you can see that the following are the most important elements of the application: definition of hypothesis/problem; significance and quality of proposed work; methodology/plans; and budget. At the end of the evaluation sheet is a section for general observations which include quality of presentation; acceptability of writing style; care in proofreading; use of excessive jargon. You should use the general observations as stylistic guidelines to the more substantive character of the proposal. Put yourself in the shoes of the reviewer to see how your proposal compares with the evaluation criteria. The application is so well constructed that close attention to the form should produce a worthy proposal. Be sure when you are done to clean it up, have it proofread by two people, and reviewed for content by at least one faculty member. Remember not to use specific field jargon.

4. Charles A. and Anne Morrow Lindbergh Grants for Research in Technology and the Preservation of the Natural/Human Environment

(Based on 2002–2003 Grants)

Administrative Agency: Lindbergh Foundation

Address: Lindbergh Foundation
   2150 Third Avenue North, Suite 310
   Anoka, MN 55303-2200
   Phone: 763-576-1596; fax: 763-576-1664
   Email: info@lindberghfoundation.org
   Web: www.lindberghfoundation.org/

Deadline and Notification: Mid-June for application submission. Award notification in April of the following year. Grants are expected to run from June 1 to May 31.

Number of Awards: 9–10 per competition.

Average Number of Applicants: 200 per competition.

Award Amount: Up to $10,580, which represents the cost of constructing Lindbergh's plane, *The Spirit of St. Louis,* in 1927.

Application Form: Online or from the above postal or email address.

Purpose of Grant/Fellowship and Restrictions: To support projects that seek to establish a balance between the preservation of the natural/human environment and advanced technology. Lindbergh's vision was "to discern nature's essential wisdom and combine it with scientific knowledge." Acceptable categories for research include: agriculture, aviation/aerospace, conservation of natural resources, education, health, and waste minimization and management. Reviewing the recent winners online gives a good indication of the types of projects funded by the foundation. Research projects related to the problems associated with tourism in environmentally sensitive areas, for example, are supported.

Length of Award: One year.

Applicant Eligibility: None specified.

Application Requirements: A completed application, which includes: two-page project summary; one- to two-page methodology description; one-page statement of projected results; budget; three-page review of the literature; personnel statement; two references. Eight copies of everything must be sent to the foundation.

Application Comments and Advice: The application is reviewed at three levels: first for how balanced the research is regarding technology and environment; and second for technical merit, which includes an assessment of the project's originality and feasibility; how well the research will solve the stated problem; how the research will contribute to our knowledge base; and whether it will make a difference in our world. Finally, those that score the best on the first and second reviews are then assessed by the full foundation board and the winners are selected. During the review process people from a variety of backgrounds may be reading the application. It is important to avoid overcomplicated jargon and technical terms that may not be understood by some of the reviewers.

In recent years, the award has become a prestigious stepping stone for important funding from other organizations. The pattern has been to select highly innovative projects in the embryonic stage. A careful review of previous winners will give you a very good sense of the types of projects that are favored. The foundation emphasizes clarity in writing. The focus is on balancing technology with the environment, so the word "balance" should be appropriately but generously used in the application.

5. Phillips Fund Grants for Native American Studies

(Based on 2002–2003 Grants)

Administrative Agency: American Philosophical Society

Address: Phillips Fund for Native American Research
   American Philosophical Society
   104 South Fifth Street
   Philadelphia, PA 19106-3387
   Phone: 215-440-3400; fax: 215-440-3436
   Web: http://amphilsoc.org/grants/phillips.htm

Deadline and Notification: March 1; award announcements in May.

Number of Awards: 19 per competition.

Award Amount: Up to $2,000 with a $1,400 average.

Application Form: Online or from the above address.

Purpose of Grant/Fellowship and Restrictions: To support research in Native American linguistics and ethnohistory, and the history of studies of native Americans in the continental U.S. and Canada. Not for archaeology, ethnography, psycholinguistics, or preparation of educational materials. Grant may be used to fund travel, tapes, films, fees, books, and equipment.

Length of Award: Research must be started within one year of award notification.

Applicant Eligibility: Master's or doctoral students at the thesis and dissertation research levels and postdoctoral scholars. Preference given to postdoctoral scholars.

Application Requirements: A completed application which includes: project description; budget; three references.

Application Comments and Advice: Since preference is given to postdoctoral scholars, the significance of the research must be great for a master's or doctoral student to win an award. Publication potential for the research should be described as should the importance of the study to the field. Patience and persistence may be needed.

6. White House and Presidential Library Travel and Research Grants

(Based on 2002–2003 Grants)

A. White House Historical Association Research Grants

Administrative Agency: White House Historical Association

Address: White House Historical Association
Research Grants Program
740 Jackson Place, NW
Washington, DC 20503
Phone: 202-737-8292; fax: 202-789-0440
Email: edu@whha.org
Web: www.whitehousehistory.org

Deadline and Notification: March 1 and September 1 for application submission; awards announced in the spring and fall.

Number of Awards: 15 per competition.

Average Number of Applicants: First application season is 2001 so no information about application numbers is available.

Award Amount: Up to $2,000.

Application Form: Online or from the above postal or email addresses.

Purpose of Grant/Fellowship and Restrictions: To support historical research that brings greater understanding of the White House. Researchers combine study at one or more of the Presidential libraries as long as the segment funded by the White House Historical Association pertains to the period when the president was living in the White House. For example, the topic proposed may be family security at the White House during the Hoover administration. The appropriate records would be located at the Hoover library and the applicant would seek funds to go to that library and review the holdings. Topics are open but those of special interest include: the image of the White House; the White House as symbol or icon; perceptions of the White House from the public, press, or foreign dignitaries; White House personnel; personnel management; Executive Residence staff; White House staff; White House permanent operating offices; administration of the White House Office; social and diplomatic functions; study of the structure and its contents; family life; communications; use of communications technology to document events; the role of the White House Press Corps; public presentation of the family.

Length of Award: One year.

Applicant Eligibility: All graduate and postdoctoral and independent projects will be considered, although preference will be given to dissertation and postdoctoral research.

Application Requirements: An application which includes: a brief description of project and final product (dissertation, book, article); two- page formal proposal; letter from the Presidential Library that verifies that the holdings to be studied are at the Library; vita; proposed budget.

Application Comments and Advice: 2001 is the first year this grant has been offered so the application numbers should be small until news about the opportunity gets around. The next few years should bring low applicant numbers and better chances of being selected for an award.

Making sure the appropriate records are located in the library and then having that verified by library staff is the most important criteria. When writing the proposal be sure to put the specific White House study within the context of the larger picture if that is appropriate. Also emphasize how the research will contribute to the body of knowledge about the White House.

For general information about all of the presidential libraries contact:

> National Archives at College Park
> 8601 Adelphi Road
> College Park, MD 20740-6001
> Phone: 301-713-6050; Fax: 301-713-6045
> Web: www.nara.gov/nara/president/address.html

The web site above provides all the addresses for the libraries plus information about hours and days open. (All the information below is based on 2002 materials)

B. George Bush Library O'Donnell and Korea Research Grants
Administrative Agency: George Bush Presidential Library Foundation
Address: George Bush Presidential Library Foundation

> Texas A & M University
> 1145 TAMU
> College Station, TX 77843-1145
> Phone: 979-862-2251; fax: 979-862-2253
> Email: nnewman@gbplc.tamu.edu
> Web: www.georgebushfoundation.org

Deadline and Notification: O'Donnell: Mid-March and mid-October for application submission; awards announced in the fall and spring. Korea: Mid-February and mid-September for application submission; fall and spring for award announcements.

Number of Awards: O'Donnell: 20–40 per competition. Korea: not available.

Average Number of Applicants: Both programs are new.

Award Amount: $500–$2,500.

Application Form: Online or from the above postal or email addresses.

Purpose of Grant/Fellowship and Restrictions: O'Donnell: To support scholarship which include topics utilizing library holdings. The award is to help cover travel, living, and research expenses. Korea: Funds are made available from the Korea Foundation to do research in the library to further the understanding of East Asia.

Length of Award: One year.

Applicant Eligibility: No specific eligibility.

Application Requirements: A completed application which includes: scope and nature of project; vita; three references; budget.

Application Comments and Advice: For both grants the library is concerned about the publication potential of the research materials and the contribution the study will make to scholarship. The applications are reviewed by a panel of scholars and administrators of the library. Specific knowledge of library holdings is key. Inquiring about special library interests regarding the Korea grant may be helpful. If this grant is to support partial research on a larger project, be sure to provide the bigger picture in the application proposal. Methodology, especially how the library materials will be approached, is important to detail in the proposal.

C. Jimmy Carter Library
Address: 453 Freedom Parkway
        Atlanta, GA 30307
        Phone: 404-420-5145
        Email: carterweb@emory.edu
        Web: www.cartercenter.org/library.html

The Carter Library does not currently offer travel grants. The White House Association does offer grants to study at the Carter Library if the topic and holdings to be used are appropriate to their requirements. See beginning of this section.

D. William J. Clinton Presidential Materials Project
Address: 1000 LaHarpe Boulevard
        Little Rock, AR 72201
        Phone: 501-244-9756; fax: 501-244-9764

Email: clinton.library@nara.gov
Web: www.clinton.nara.gov

At this writing the Clinton Foundation has been established and can be accessed through the above addresses. The library is now in the design phase. When the library is built, research will be allowed by appointment only. It remains to be seen if travel grants will be available.

E. The Eisenhower Presidential Library Abilene Travel Grants Program
Administrative Agency: The Eisenhower Foundation
Address: Abilene Travel Grants Program
Eisenhower Foundation
c/o Dwight D. Eisenhower Library
200 SE Fourth Street
Abilene, KS 67410
Phone: 877-RINGIKE; fax: 785-263-4218
Email: eisenhower.library@nara.gov
Web: www.eisenhower.utexas.edu

Deadline and Notification: Late February for application submission for spring review and late September for application submission for fall review. Award notification around six weeks after application deadline.

Number of Awards: 10–20 per year.

Average Number of Applicants: 20–40 per year.

Award Amount: Up to $1,000.

Application Form: Online or from the above postal and email addresses.

Purpose of Grant/Fellowship and Restrictions: To support travel to the library to do research in history, government, economics, communications, and international affairs. The grants support work leading to a book, dissertation, thesis, article, or other endeavor which contributes to the knowledge base.

Length of Award: Travel must occur within one year of the award.

Applicant Eligibility: None stated.

Application Requirements: Completed application which includes: letter from a library archivist confirming availability of relevant materials; vita; summary of five pages or less on subject and scope of project; travel timetable; ten- to fifteen-page writing sample; budget; information on any other grants received for the project; two or three letters of recommendation; intended publication or other use of the research.

Application Comments and Advice: Preparation done through the library is key to this grant. When writing the proposal, be sure to put the library investigation within the context of the larger picture if that is appropriate. Because the program is concerned that the research "may provide informed leadership in our national life," be sure to address that interest. That could mean, for example, the study will be submitted to a journal like *Foreign Policy* and could help shape opinions in the Department of State where it will certainly be read.

F. Gerald R. Ford Foundation Travel Grants
Administrative Agency: Gerald R. Ford Library
Address: Grants Coordinator
      Gerald R. Ford Library
      1000 Beal Avenue
      Ann Arbor, MI 48109
      Phone: 734-741-2218; fax: 734-741-2341
      Email: ford.library@nara.gov
      Web: www.ford.utexas.edu/library/hpgrants.htm
Deadline and Notification: Mid-March and mid-September for application submission. Award notification six to eight weeks after the deadline.
Award Amount: Up to $2,000.
Number of Awards: 10–20 per competition. The foundation authorizes $20,000 a year for grant support. No award is larger than $2,000.
Average Number of Applicants: 30–35 per competition.
Application Form: Online or from the above postal and email addresses.
Purpose of Grant/Fellowship and Restrictions: To support research primarily in the fields of federal policies and institutions, politics in the 1970s with special interest in the library's holding strengths in domestic affairs and policies, the 1970 presidential election, media relations, White House management and decision making, congressional relations, foreign policy.
Length of Award: Awardee must begin research within one year of receiving an award notice.
Applicant Eligibility: None stated.
Application Requirements: Completed application which includes: a form; vita; two–three page summary of proposed project; three recommendations.
Application Comments and Advice: Be sure to contact the archives staff and determine what holdings are available and appropriate to your research. Include in the proposal with whom contact has been made and what materials are in the library and important to the research. An online list of "Recent Grant Recipients and Their Topics" gives a sense of what the foundation is supporting. Be sure to review this list.

G. Herbert Hoover Library Travel Grants
Administrative Agency: Herbert Hoover Presidential Library
Address: Chairman, Fellowship and Grant Committee
      Hoover Presidential Library Association

PO Box 696
West Branch, IA 52358
Phone: 319-643-5327; fax: 319-643-2391
Email: info@hooverassociation.org
Web: www.hoover.nara.gov

Deadline and Notification: March 1 for application submission; May 1 for award announcements.

Number of Awards: Up to 20 per competition.

Award Amount: $500–$1,500.

Application Form: Online or from the above postal or email address.

Purpose of Grant/Fellowship and Restrictions: To support research at the library in the areas "of interest to Herbert Hoover, Lou Henry Hoover, their associates and other public figures as reflected in the Library's collection."

Length of Award: Must be completed within twelve months of the May 15 after the award announcement.

Applicant Eligibility: None stated.

Application Requirements: Completed application form which includes: project proposal; bibliography; vita; three letters of recommendation; budget.

Application Comments and Advice: Contact the archives staff to determine what holdings are appropriate for the research. Be sure to mention the name of the staff member and the specific holdings in the proposal.

H. Lyndon Baines Johnson Foundation Research Grants

Administrative Agency: Lyndon Baines Johnson Library and Museum

Address: Lyndon Baines Johnson Library and Museum
2313 Red River Street
Austin, TX 78705
Phone: 512-916-5137
Email: johnson.library@nara.gov
Web: www.lbjlib.utexas.edu

Deadline: February 28 and August 31 for application submission.

Number of Awards: 10–20 per competition.

Average Number of Applicants: 15–40 per competition.

Award Amount: $500–$2,000; a separate $250 is available for photocopying for students residing within a fifty-mile radius.

Application Form: Available from the supervisory archivist at the above postal address. The current supervisory archivist is Tina Houston, tina.houston@johnson.nara.gov.

Purpose of Grant/Fellowship and Restrictions: To support research in the archives, which contain 44 million documents, audiovisual materials, and oral interviews with 1,000 people. Johnson's papers include:

White House files, 1963–1969; U.S. Congressman files, 1937–1949; U.S. Senator files, 1949–1961; Vice Presidential files, 1961–1963.
Length of Award: None stated.
Applicant Eligibility: None stated.
Application Requirements: Completed application.
Application Comments and Advice: Since there are so many materials in the archives, plenty of preparation is needed before applying for this grant.

I. John F. Kennedy Library Research Grants
Administrative Agency: John F. Kennedy Library
Address: Grants and Fellowship Coordinator
John F. Kennedy Library
Columbia Point
Boston, MA 02125
Phone: 877-616-4599 *or* 617-929-4500; fax: 617-929-4538
Email: kennedy.library@nara.gov
Web: www.jfklibrary.org
Deadline and Notification: March 15 and August 15 for application submission: April 20 and October 20 for award notification.
Number of Awards: 15–20 per competition.
Award Amount: $500–$2,500.
Application Form: Online or from the postal and email addresses above.
Purpose of Grant/Fellowship and Restrictions: To support research in the library of Kennedy period studies. Preference is given to Ph.D. candidates and recent postdocs working in "newly opened or relatively unused collections." Also to recent Ph.D. recipients who are expanding dissertations for publication.
Length of Award: None stated.
Applicant Eligibility: None stated.
Application Requirements: Completed application which includes: letter memo describing research, outcomes, significance; three letters of recommendation; ten-page writing sample; budget; vita.
Application Comments and Advice: Preference will be given to those not supported by large grants from elsewhere. A visit with an archivist should be made to determine available resource materials and to see how newly opened the information is or how utilized the resources are.

J. Richard M. Nixon Holdings at the Library and in the National Archives
Address: Richard M. Nixon Library and Birthplace
The Archives
18001 Yorba Linda Boulevard
Yorba Linda, CA 92886

Phone: 714-993-5075, ext. 209
Web: www.nixonfoundation.org/archives.shtml
and   Nixon Presidential Materials Staff
National Archives at College Park
8601 Adelphi Road
College Park, MD 20740-6001
Phone: 301-713-6950; fax: 301-713-6916
Email: nixon@nara.gov

The Nixon documents are located in the two places listed above. The pre- and post-presidential papers are located in the library. The presidential years resources are at the National Archives by an act of Congress relative to the Watergate investigation. No funding is available to travel to these collections.

K. Ronald Reagan Presidential Library
Address: Ronald Reagan Library
40 Presidential Drive
Simi Valley, CA 93065
Phone: 800-410-8354; fax: 805-522-9621
Email: reagan.library@nara.gov
Web: www.reagan.utexas.edu

No grants available at this writing.

L. Franklin and Eleanor Roosevelt Institute Grants
Administrative Agency: The Roosevelt Institute
Address: Chairman, Grants Committee
Franklin and Eleanor Roosevelt Institute
4079 Albany Post Road
Hyde Park, NY 12538
Phone: 845-229-8114; fax: 845-229-0872
Email: roosevelt.library@nara.gov
Web: www.fdrlibrary.marist.edu/rgrants.html

Deadline and Notification: February 15 and September 15 for application submission. Awards announced are in the spring and fall.
Number of Awards: 10–15 per competition.
Average Number of Applicants: 20–24 per competition.
Award Amount: Up to $2,500.
Application Form: Online or from the above postal and email addresses.
Purpose of Grant/Fellowship and Restrictions: To encourage younger scholars to do research on the "Roosevelt Years" and especially the areas of emerging democracies and the Third World. The grants are for travel to and use of Roosevelt archival material.
Length of Award: Varies.

Applicant Eligibility: None stated.

Application Requirements: Completed application which includes: two-page or less research proposal; stated relevance of archival materials to the proposal; schedule of travel to Library; bibliography of works applicant has published; vita; budget; three letters of reference.

Application Comments and Advice: Pre-application contact with a staff archivist is important since staff will evaluate the application. Be sure to put your proposal within the bigger research picture if that is appropriate. Also indicate the significance of the project to the Roosevelt body of knowledge.

M. Harry S Truman Library Institute Research Grants and Dissertation Year Fellowships

Administrative Agency: Harry S Truman Library

Address: Harry S Truman Library Institute
　　　　Grants Administrator
　　　　500 West U.S. Highway 24
　　　　Independence, MO 64050
　　　　Phone: 800-833-1225 *or* 816-833-1400; fax: 816-833-4368
　　　　Email: truman.library@nara.gov
　　　　Web: www.trumanlibrary.org

Deadlines and Notification: For Research Grant: April 1 and October 1 for application submission; award notification about six weeks after deadline. For Dissertation Year Fellowship: February 1 for application submission; award notification four weeks after deadline.

Number of Awards: 20 per competition; 19–20 for graduate student and postdoctoral Research Grant; 1 or 2 for Dissertation Year Fellowship.

Average Number of Applicants: 60 for Research Grant; 6–10 for Dissertation Year Fellowship.

Award Amount: Up to $2,500 for Research Grant; $16,000 for Dissertation Year Fellowship.

Application Form: From the above addresses.

Purpose of Grant/Fellowship and Restrictions: The Research Grant is awarded to graduate students and postdocs for travel to the library to study the holdings for one to three weeks. The Dissertation Year Fellowship is to support one year of dissertation writing on a topic related to Harry S Truman, his life and career, or the issues that were important during his presidency. Travel to the library is not expected nor required.

Length of Award: One to three weeks of library study with the Research Grant. One year of dissertation writing with the Dissertation Year Fellowship.

Applicant Eligibility: The Research Grant is available to any applicant, but preference is given to graduate students and postdoctoral scholars whose work has the highest likelihood of publication. An applicant may receive no more than two research grants in five years. Applicants for the Dissertation Year Fellowship must be at the writing stage. Applicants who have made extensive use of the library holdings will be favored.

Application Requirements: Research Grant: completed application which includes: vita; two letters of reference; project description and justification of five pages or less; list of specific files to be used at the library; name of archivist contacted; budget.

For Dissertation Year Fellowship: vita; dissertation prospectus; time schedule for completion; two letters of recommendation.

Application Comments and Advice: The Research Grant requires contact with the archives so do that first. Also a detailed listing of the documents to be used is required. Be sure to put the project to be done at the library within the context of the larger picture if that is appropriate. Be sure to detail the publication potential of your work and what it will significantly contribute to the body of knowledge about Truman. If you have not done any work at the library, contact them to make sure it is worth applying for the Dissertation Year Fellowship. Be sure to read the recent awards list provided with the application to get a sense of the topics funded.

7. Sigma Xi Research Grants

(Based on 2002–2003 Grants)
Administrative Agency: Sigma Xi, The Scientific Research Society
Address: Committee on Grants-in-Aid of Research
   Sigma Xi, The Scientific Research Society
   PO Box 13975
   Research Triangle Park, NC 27709
   Phone: 800-243-6534 *or* 919-549-4691; fax: 919-549-0090
   Email: giar@sigmaxi.org
   Web: www.sigmaxi.org
Deadline and Notification: Mid-March and mid-October for application submission. Award announcement twelve weeks after the deadline.
Number of Awards: 300 per competition.
Average Number of Applicants: 1,000 per competition.
Award Amount: For projects restricted to Society membership (see below) up to $1,000 (average of $600). For projects in the open fund where membership in the Society is not required: up to $2,500 for astronomy, vision research; up to $5,000 for Plasma Fund research.
Application Form: Online.
Purpose of Grant/Fellowship and Restrictions: The grant is restricted to

Society membership and supports undergraduate and graduate student investigations in any field. The open funds are to support research in astronomy, vision, and plasma issues such as safety of the blood supply worldwide.

Length of Award: Depends on the project.

Applicant Eligibility: The restricted grants require that the faculty advisor or the student applicant be a member of the Society prior to deadline. Students must be enrolled in a degree program.

Application Requirements: A completed application which includes: data on the faculty advisor who will oversee the project; two recommendations (one is the faculty advisor); 400-word research proposal (any more will not be read); location of research (travel can be part of the funding); budget.

Application Comments and Advice: This is a straightforward, simple application. You need to work with your faculty advisor on the construction of the proposal and the budget.

8. Social Science Research Council (SSRC) Predissertation Fellowships in Applied Economics

(Based on 2002–2003 Fellowships)

Administrative Agency: SSRC

Address: Program in Applied Economics
　　　　　SSRC
　　　　　810 Seventh Avenue, 31st Floor
　　　　　New York, NY 10019
　　　　　Phone: 212-377-2700, ext. 502; fax: 212-377-2727
　　　　　Email: pae@ssrc.org
　　　　　Web: www.ssrc.org

Deadline and Notification: February 1 for application submission; award announcements in May.

Number of Awards: 12–15 per competition.

Average Number of Applicants: 65–70 per competition.

Award Amount: $15,000.

Application Form: Online or from the above addresses.

Purpose of Grant/Fellowship and Restrictions: To support economics doctoral students bridge the transition from course work to dissertation research by helping them develop new skills in theoretical and empirical understanding of real-world problems. The idea is to enhance these skills outside the department by innovative methods which might, for example, include internships in agencies or institutes, or interdisciplinary work.

Length of Award: One year.

Applicant Eligibility: Full-time enrollment in a U.S. economics doctoral program. Completion of course work and qualifying examinations prior to award announcement; usually third-year students. Preference given to alumni of SSRC Summer Workshop in Applied Economics.

Application Requirements: A completed application, which includes a summary of potential dissertation topic and three references who can attest to the importance and scope of the proposed topic and qualifications of the applicant to carry out the proposal.

Application Comments and Advice: SSRC is looking for innovative and dynamic new ways "to address vital and complex economic and social issues." Be sure to read the list of past fellows and projects and seriously consider the summer workshop.

Chapter 6
Dissertation Fellowships and Grants

This chapter provides general information and application writing advice for dissertation fellowship and grant applications. It also describes in detail specific funding opportunities, namely:

1. American Council of Learned Societies (ACLS) Dissertation Fellowships in American Art and Eastern European Studies
2. American Association of University Women (AAUW) American Dissertation Fellowships and Selected Professions Fellowships
3. Ford Foundation Dissertation Fellowships for Minorities
4. Harry Frank Guggenheim Foundation Ph.D. Dissertation Fellowships
5. National Science Foundation (NSF) Grants for Improving Doctoral Dissertation Research
6. Charlotte W. Newcombe Doctoral Dissertation Fellowships
7. Spencer Foundation Dissertation Year Fellowships
8. Social Science Research Council (SSRC) Fellowships
   A. International Dissertation Field Research Program
   B. Berlin Program for Advanced German and European Studies
   C. Program on Philanthropy and the Nonprofit Sector
   D. Sexuality Research Fellowship Program
9. Woodrow Wilson Foundation Dissertation Grants in Women's Studies and Women's and Children's Health

Fields funded by one or more of these fellowships are behavioral and social sciences, humanities, sciences, engineering, and public health.

General Information

Dissertation grants may be awarded to support thesis research and/or writing. Some competitions require that ABD (all but dissertation) status be achieved just prior to application. Others require that the applicant be ABD just prior to receiving the award.

Dissertation funding comes in a variety of types. Some have been established to support groups of people who have not been historically well supported by universities, such as women and minorities. Fellowships such as the AAUW and the Ford fall into this category.

Another type of dissertation award is designed to support students in a specific disciplinary area. The NSF grant, for example, funds work in biological sciences. Still a third type supports work in specific research areas. The Guggenheim dissertation fellowships are made available to those who do work in the areas of violence, aggression, and dominance. Other dissertation support is for research abroad, some of which is described in Chapter 4.

Dissertation funding can provide money for cost of living, travel, supplies, and equipment. Some fellowships provide small amounts of money while others are quite generous. Be sure to see Chapter 5, Research Grants, for other opportunities that may be used to fund dissertation work.

The initial stage of dissertation proposal preparation is the time to start the search for grants. Support can be especially important to students who have outlived their institutional funding and must rely on outside money.

A dissertation fellowship is a very good credential that appeals to employment search committees. It shows your assertiveness and organization and is a recognition of the quality of your research. A student who wins research and dissertation grants during his or her graduate school days is viewed as more likely to secure such funding in the future. That is a real plus on a job application. In some fields like anthropology, it is a serious requirement.

If your proposal is rejected, be sure to reapply. Not all agencies allow reapplication so check the rules. Those that do will usually supply reviewer's remarks if requested to do so. These opinions can be helpful in redirecting the proposal revision; other times evaluations are useless. Until you see them, you cannot know how helpful they will be, so request a copy whenever you consider reapplication.

It is important to determine whether your project will be of interest to a particular agency. Sometimes you can figure that out by reviewing a list of past winning topics. The Guggenheim, for example, gives a list of past winners, their university affiliations, and their topics, for the past three years. Many agencies have this available online. In some cases it is prudent to email or call an agency and find out if a topic is suitable. NSF is particularly good at guiding students with regard to fields and areas of studies in which they have particular interests. Most organizations are interested in getting the most relevant applications so they are usually very helpful to students who make contact. If you have questions after reading the information/application information, a call or email can save you a lot of aggravation and wasted time.

Application Advice

1. *Begin looking for fellowships when starting to write the dissertation proposal.* The proposal writing stage is a good time to ask faculty and more advanced students what is available in the field. If the department or administration has someone who helps students locate funding opportunities, schedule a visit to his or her office. Since money is available for the various stages of dissertation work, it is helpful to know early on what is available.
2. *Do not apply for anything until after selecting your dissertation director.* Most agencies rely heavily upon the opinion of the faculty advisor when evaluating proposals. If your dissertation director is not wild with enthusiasm about the project, the likelihood of doing well in a fellowship competition is limited.
3. *Do not just attach the dissertation proposal to every application and hope for the best.* Each application is different. Although most agencies want substantially the same information, the order of presentation and amount of space permitted always varies. Additionally, you may want funding to support a specific part of your research and that area should be emphasized. Be very willing to tailor your research project description to the requirements of each individual application. Fine tuning takes more time, but the results are worth it.
4. *Do seriously consider reapplication if an application is rejected.* This is especially true for study abroad fellowships. Six months' or a year's worth of research always improves focus and usually results in a better application effort.
5. *Know when to borrow money.* For some, there comes a point when time is better spent finishing the dissertation than sending out more funding applications. At that point, seeking external funding becomes more trouble than it is worth. The fellowship-seeking process can help to focus and facilitate the research, but at some point it can interrupt the flow of research or writing. In the long run, it may make better economic sense to finish the degree and concentrate on finding a job or writing a postdoctoral fellowship application. The decision is an individual call and should be made in consultation with a faculty advisor and a financial aid administrator.

Specific Fellowship Opportunities

All information, except the author's advice, is taken from the actual application information, award announcements, web sites and other documents written by the agencies, and on contact made with each agency. Every effort is made to use the same language as that on the application or to paraphrase or summarize that language. For ease of reading, quotation marks are used only to draw special attention to important application sections.

1. American Council of Learned Societies (ACLS) Dissertation Fellowships in American Art History and Eastern European Studies

(Based on 2001–2002 Fellowships)
Administrative Agency: American Council of Learned Societies
Address: American Council of Learned Societies
       228 East 45th Street
       New York, NY 10017-3398
       Phone: 212-697-1505; fax: 212-949-8058
       Email: karen@acls.org
       Web: www.acls.org
Deadline and Notification: American Art History: mid-November for application deadline; early April for award announcement. Eastern European Studies: November 1 for application submission; late April for award announcement.
Number of Awards: 10 for American Art History, 10 for Eastern European Studies, per competition.
Average Number of Applications: 60–70 for American Art History; 60–70 for Eastern European Studies, per competition.
Award Amount: $20,000 for American Art; $15,000 for Eastern European Studies.
Application Form: Online or from above address.
Purpose of Grant/Fellowship and Restrictions: American Art History: to support dissertation work in the art history of the United States in any period. Dissertation research or writing is funded. The fellowship is not renewable.

Eastern European Studies: To support dissertation research and writing in the social sciences and humanities pertaining to Albania, Baltic Republics, Bulgaria, Czech Republic, Hungary, Poland, Romania, Slovakia, and the successor states of Yugoslavia.
Length of Award: One year.
Applicant Eligibility: American Art History: U.S. citizen; doctoral students

in an art history department (although degree may be sought in another department if the primary dissertation advisor is in the art history department). The topic should be object-oriented and in the visual arts. All requirements but the dissertation completed before the award period (June following application) begins.

Eastern European Studies: U.S. citizen or permanent resident; willingness to devote one academic year to dissertation work only.

2. American Association of University Women (AAUW) American Dissertation Fellowship and Selected Professions Fellowships

(Based on 2002–2003 Fellowships)
Administrative Agency: American Association of University Women
Address: AAUW
        111 Sixteenth Street, NW
        Washington, D.C. 20036
        Phone: 319-337-1716
        Email: foundation@aauw.org
        Web: www.aauw.org

AAUW American Fellowships
Deadline: Mid-November for application submission; award notification in early May.
Number of Awards: 51 per competition.
Average Number of Applications: 914 per competition.
Award Amount: $20,000.
Application Form: Online or from the address above. Applications available in August through November 1.
Purpose of Grant/Fellowship and Restrictions: To support one year of dissertation writing for women doctoral candidates in all fields except engineering (see Selected Professions Fellowships below). Of special interest is research in gender issues.
Length of Award: One year.
Applicant Eligibility: U.S citizens or permanent residents. Women only. Completion of all course work and exams and have an accepted dissertation proposal by the application deadline.
Application Requirements: A completed application.
Application Comments and Advice: AAUW is very interested in academic achievement, teaching experience, and "active commitment to helping women and girls through service in their communities, professions, or fields of research." Applications will be evaluated to a great extent on the above criteria.

Since the fields are wide open for this competition, you can be assured that someone from outside your area will review and evaluate your application. Be sure to stay away from disciplinary jargon and write the proposal section in a clear, straightforward manner that can be understood by a highly intelligent person not necessarily in your field.

AAUW Selected Professions Fellowships: Master's and First Professional Awards and Engineering Dissertation Awards

Deadline: Master's and First Professional: January 10 for application submission. Engineering Dissertation: November 15 for application submission; award notification in early May.

Number of Awards: Master's and First Professional: 32; Engineering Dissertation: 11, per competition.

Average Number of Applications: Master's and First Professional: 177; Engineering Dissertation: 26, per competition.

Award Amount: Master's and First Professional: $5,000–$12,000; Engineering Dissertation: $20,000.

Application Form: Online or from the above address.

Purpose of Grant/Fellowship and Restrictions: Master's and First Professional: to support women in degree programs where they have been underrepresented. Support is for the final year of study in master's degree programs in architecture; computer/information sciences; mathematics/statistics. Engineering master's students may apply for their first or third year of study.

Women of color in master's programs in business administration; J.D. programs in law; M.D. programs in medicine (third or fourth year) are also eligible to apply.

Engineering Dissertation

Purpose of Grant/Fellowship and Restrictions: To support the final dissertation writing year.

Length of Award: One year.

Applicant Eligibility: U.S. citizen or permanent resident.

Application Requirements: Completed application.

Application Comments and Advice: The purpose is to support women in fields in which they have been underrepresented. Pay close attention to eligibility with regard to which years of course work are covered. It is different for several fields. Certainly high achievement is a fundamental consideration so grades should be outstanding. Interest in gender issues and support within the community of women and girls is important to this organization. Be sure to included descriptions or any volunteer work done regarding these groups.

3. Ford Foundation Dissertation Fellowships for Minorities

(Based on 2002–2003 Fellowships)
Administrative Agency: National Research Council
Address: Fellowship Office/FD, TJ 2041
　　　　　National Research Council
　　　　　2001 Wisconsin Avenue, NW
　　　　　Washington, DC 20007
　　　　　Phone: 202-334-2872; fax: 202-334-3419
　　　　　Email: infofell@nas.edu
　　　　　Web: http://national-academies.org/osep/fo
Deadline and Notification: December 1 for application submission; award
　notification in April.
Number of Awards: 40 per competition.
Average Number of Applications: 200–300 per competition.
Award Amount: $24,000; expenses paid to attend three conferences for
　fellows.
Application Form: Online after August 1 or from address above.
Purpose of Grant/Fellowship and Restrictions: To increase the number of
　unrepresented minorities in U.S. university and college life for the
　following groups: Alaskan Natives; Black/African Americans; Mexi-
　can American/Chicanas/Chinanos; Native American Indians; Native
　Pacific Islanders (Polynesians and Micronesians); and Puerto Ricans.
　Applicants must be students enrolled in Ph.D. or Sc.D. programs in
　the following fields: behavior and social sciences, humanities, engi-
　neering, mathematics, physical sciences, life sciences, and education,
　or interdisciplinary programs within two of the above areas.
Length of Award: 9–12 months.
Applicant Eligibility: U.S. citizen or national; member of one of the
　above groups; enrollment in a Ph.D. or Sc.D. program in one of the
　above disciplines career; aim of teaching or research in an academic
　venue.
Application Requirements: Completed application which includes: docu-
　mentation of candidacy by mid-February of application season; four
　references that include the dissertation advisor; statement of long-
　range career goals; dissertation abstract; plan for completion of the
　doctoral degree; transcripts.
Application Comments and Advice: The Ford program is looking for an
　absolute commitment on the part of applicants to pursue a career in
　teaching and/or research at U.S. colleges or universities. It is impor-
　tant to really think this through and visualize an academic career that
　includes the encouragement of other minority students in the pursuit

of like academic careers. This program hopes to foster role models to increase campus diversity and right the wrongs of historic discrimination and under representation in academia.

Potential to finish the degree is another important criterion for evaluation. Since a high percentage of students who begin doctoral programs do not complete them, the Ford Program wants real assurance that the applicant has a plan and timetable to completion. You need to be very positive, organized, and convincing in this area, especially students in the humanities where many students fall by the wayside at the dissertation stage and where the dissertation can drag on for four or more years.

This is a long application, but working through it can help crystallize and organize the dissertation plan. It is well worth the effort.

4. Harry Frank Guggenheim Foundation Ph.D. Dissertation Fellowships

(Based on 2002–2003 Fellowships)
Administrative Agency: Harry Frank Guggenheim Foundation
Address: Harry Frank Guggenheim Foundation
　　　　527 Madison Avenue
　　　　New York, NY 10022-4304
　　　　Phone: 212-644-4907; fax: 212-644-5110
　　　　Web: www.hfg.org
Deadline and Notification: February 1 for application submission; award notification in June.
Number of Awards: 10 per competition.
Average Number of Applications: 200 per competition.
Award Amount: $10,000.
Application Form: Online or from the above address.
Purpose of Grant/Fellowship and Restrictions: To support the final dissertation writing year of students in the natural and social sciences and humanities. Research should address and increase the "understanding of the causes, manifestations, and control of violence, aggression, and dominance." Projects that increase the understanding as well as propose solutions to the abatement of violence, aggression and dominance will receive highest consideration. Of special interest are the following topics: social change, the socialization of children, intergroup conflict, interstate warfare, crime, family relationships, and control of aggression and violence. The research must be useful. Areas and methods not funded by other resources will receive special attention.

Length of Award: One year.

Applicant Eligibility: Ph.D. candidates in final year. Any nationality is eligible, as are students enrolled in any university worldwide.

Application Requirements: A completed application which includes: abstract in English; dissertation advisor letter; four copies of the research plan; human subjects protection guarantee.

Application Comments and Advice: In "A Special Note to Applicants for the Dissertation Fellowship" the agency warns that any application that is disorganized, incomplete, and a chore to read will not have much of a chance. The message seems to be that many applications arrive in that state and the readers are tired of it. So be warned. The biggest mistakes made by applicants as listed by the agency are the following: applicant will not finish the dissertation in the grant year; project is not directly relevant to violence, aggression, or dominance; only one copy arrives; application is late; advisor's letter and c.v. arrive separately and/or late and/or only one copy is sent; some key part is missing like research plan, or abstract; the note on other support has been ignored. As with any other fellowship you apply for, the rules must be read and followed carefully.

5. National Science Foundation (NSF) Grants for Improving Doctoral Dissertation Research

(Based on 2002–2003 Fellowships)

Administrative Agency: National Science Foundation

Address: NSF

        4201 Wilson Blvd.

        Arlington, VA 22230

        Phone: 703-292-8480 Division of Environmental Biology

        Phone: 703-292-8420 Division of Integrative Biology and Neurosciences

        Email: pubs@nsf.gov

        Web: www.nsf.gov

Deadline and Notification: Third Friday in November for application submission; award notification within six months of deadline.

Number of Awards: 80–90 per competition.

Award Amount: $3,000–$10,000.

Application Form: Online or from the above address.

Purpose of Grant/Fellowship and Restrictions: To support dissertation-level students whose research falls into the scope of the Division of Environmental Biology (DEP), Animal Behavior or Ecological and Evolutionary Physiology programs in the Division of Integrative Biology and

Neurosciences (IBN). The award is for supplemental items like travel to facilities or field research locations, data collection, and use of research facilities. The application must be submitted through the institution by the dissertation director on behalf of the student. Does not support disease-related research or marine ecology.

Length of Award: Can be used over a period of two years.

Applicant Eligibility: A Ph.D. student who has advanced to candidacy. No citizenship requirements.

Application Requirements: Completed application which includes: project summary (limit 200 words); project description (limit eight single-spaced pages); budget and justification; submission through the Fast-Lane system.

Application Comments and Advice: Proposals are reviewed by three people outside the NSF with field expertise using the following criteria: What is the intellectual merit of the proposed activity? What are the broader impacts of the proposed activity? Does the proposed research integrate research and education? Does the research integrate diversity into NSF programs, projects, and activities?

The proposal information elaborates on the above evaluation guidelines which should be carefully read. Additional information is available through contacts at NSF in the two directorates listed above.

6. Charlotte W. Newcombe Doctoral Dissertation Fellowships

(Based on 2002–2003 Fellowships)
Administrative Agency: Woodrow Wilson National Fellowship Foundation
Address: Charlotte W. Newcombe Fellowships
Woodrow Wilson National Fellowship Foundation
CN 5281
Princeton, NJ 08543-5281
Phone: 609-452-7007; fax: 609-452-0066
Email: charlotte@woodrow.org
Web: http://www.woodrow.org/newcombe

Deadline and Notification: Late November for outside of U.S. application submission; early December for in U.S. application submission; award notification in April.

Number of Awards: 35 per competition.

Average Number of Applications: 400 per competition.

Award Amount: $16,500.

Application Form: Online or from the above addresses.

Purpose of Grant/Fellowship and Restrictions: To support dissertation writing on topics where the thesis central core is comprised of original and significant research in the areas of ethical or religious values in all fields of the humanities and social sciences. Topics include, for example, "the ethical implications of foreign policy and the values influencing political decisions, the moral codes of other cultures," and "religious or ethical issues reflected in history or literature."

Length of Award: One year of full-time dissertation writing.

Applicant Eligibility: Candidates who have completed all requirements except the dissertation in Ph.D. or Th.D. programs in the U.S.; candidates who are at the writing stage when the award begins and who expect to complete the dissertation at the end of the award year.

Application Requirements: Completed application which includes: three letters of recommendation including the dissertation director; dissertation abstract; proposal (limit six pages); timetable for degree completion.

Application Comments and Advice: Since you cannot reapply for this fellowship, be sure the timing is right before submitting. Be very clear about the focus of this fellowship before applying. The emphasis is on sweeping questions of ethics and religious ideas and how these effect people's lives, especially in the choices they make. Although any time period can be investigated, the issues need to be those that have continued to impact people over time.

The applications will be read by a wide spectrum of academics so proposal language should be clear, concise, and lacking in disciplinary jargon. The review committee will read the dissertation abstract first along with the eligibility requirements. They will review no further if they are not impressed. Be sure the abstract hits the central premise of the fellowship or it will be a waste of time.

7. Spencer Foundation Dissertation Year Fellowships

(Based on 2002–2003 Fellowship)

Administrative Agency: Spencer Foundation

Address: Spencer Dissertation Fellowships Program
       Spencer Foundation
       875 North Michigan Avenue, Suite 3930
       Chicago, IL 60611-1803
       Phone: 312-274-6526; fax: 312-337-0282
       Email: fellows@spencer.org
       Web: www.spencer.org

Deadline and Notification: Applications available July 1 until early October; application submission mid-October; award notification April; award tenure begins June 1.

Number of Awards: 35 per competition.

Average Number of Applications: 600 per competition.

Award Amount: $20,000.

Application Form: Online or from the above address.

Purpose of Grant/Fellowship and Restrictions: To support dissertation work that "show potential for bringing fresh and constructive perspectives to the history, theory, or practice of formal or informal education anywhere in the world." Field of study is open to the arts and sciences as well as professional disciplines. A future career in which education is a research topic is important.

Length of Award: The fellowship may be used over a two-year period in accordance with a submitted timetable. The idea is not to support data collection but the final analysis of the data and writing of the dissertation.

Applicant Eligibility: Doctoral candidacy reached by the time the award period begins; enrollment at a U.S. university; no citizenship requirement.

Application Requirements: A completed application which includes: statement (limit 500 words) about academic background, how the dissertation topic was selected, and future research interests; dissertation abstract; proposal (limit 1,750 words); dissertation director recommendation; faculty member letter of recommendation.

Application Comments and Advice: A wide range of disciplines will be represented on the review committee, so be sure to avoid disciplinary jargon. Review the list of topics that have been funded to see if yours fits the mold. Interdisciplinary topics are of great interest. Improvement of education is the goal of the foundation. Topics previously funded range from "the impact of high-stakes testing and grade retention on student achievement in Chicago" to "the history curricula of India, Pakistan, and Bangladesh." If you have any questions about how well your topic meets the foundation's requirements, be sure to contact the foundation. The odds are pretty long on winning an award, so be sure your area of research is a very good fit.

8. Social Science Research Council (SSRC)

(Based on 2002–2003 Fellowships)

The SSRC funds four dissertation fellowship programs:
   A. International Dissertation Field Research Program
   B. Berlin Program for Advanced German and European Studies
   C. Program on Philanthropy and the Nonprofit Sector
   D. Sexuality Research Fellowship Program

A. SSRC International Dissertation Field Research Program

Address: International Dissertation Field Research Fellowship
         Social Science Research Council

810 Seventh Avenue
New York, NY 10019
Phone: 212-377-2700, ext. 616; fax: 212-377-2727
Email: idrf@ssrc.org
Web: www.ssrc.org

Deadline and Notification: Early November for application submission; award announcements in April.

Number of Awards: 50 per competition.

Average Number of Applications: 700 per competition.

Award Amount: Up to $16,000.

Application Form: Online or from the above addresses.

Purpose of Grant/Fellowship and Restrictions: To support dissertation field research in all areas and regions of the world outside of the United States for humanities and social sciences. Fellows will also participate in post-award multidisciplinary workshops and networking sessions as part of the awards program.

Length of Award: Nine to twelve months of field research.

Applicant Eligibility: Full-time enrollment in a doctoral program at a U.S. university; all requirements of a Ph.D. except dissertation must be met by the time fellowship begins.

Application Requirements: A completed application that includes: seven copies of the application; transcripts; letter of institutional affiliation abroad (not required but preferred); three letters of recommendation; language evaluation if necessary.

Application Comments and Advice: Be sure to consult the SSRC's "Art of Writing Proposals" for guidance. This award is seen as encouragement to exceptional candidates whose research "can inform debates that go beyond the specific topic and place chosen for study." Another section of the SSRC literature refers to studies addressing issues "that transcend their disciplines or area specializations." This is a call for big picture, important work, and your proposal must address this requirement directly.

B. SSRC Berlin Program for Advanced German and European Studies at the Freie Universitat Berlin

Administrative Agency: Social Science Research Council

Address: SSRC
810 Seventh Avenue
New York, NY 10019
Phone: 212-377-2700; fax: 212-377-2727
Email: berlin@ssrc.org
Web: www.ssrc.org

Deadline and Notification: December 1 for application submission; award notifications in mid-May.

Number of Awards: 6 per competition.

Average Number of Applications: 90 per competition.

Award Amount: 2000DM a month for single person; 2500DM a month for awardee and spouse; a round-trip ticket to Berlin; intra-European research travel allowance if needed.

Application Form: Online or from the above addresses.

Purpose of Grant/Fellowship and Restrictions: To support dissertation research that is comparative and interdisciplinary in economics and the political and social aspects of contemporary Germany and Europe. Fields eligible include: anthropology; economics; political science; sociology; history; and culture studies.

Length of Award: Nine to twelve months.

Applicant Eligibility: U.S. and Canadian citizens and permanent residents; completion of all doctoral requirements except the dissertation when award begins.

Application Requirements: Completed application which includes: proposal and bibliography (limit twelve pages); summary of research locations; justification for study in Germany; language evaluation; three recommendations; academic transcripts.

Application Comments and Advice: Be sure to review "The Art of Writing the Proposal" section on the SSRC web site for clues on preparing your applications. The council is looking for groundbreaking work in methodology and theory of an interdisciplinary nature. Be sure to address this requirement. They advise not to write the proposal in disciplinary jargon because it will be read by an interdisciplinary group of reviewers. Be sure the proposal is "realistic in scope, clearly formulated, and responsive to theoretical and methodological concerns." If your language skills are not up to speed, provide a formula for how they will be so by the time you start the award period.

C. SSRC Program on Philanthropy and the Nonprofit Sector

Administrative Agency: Social Science Research Council

Address: SSRC

> Program on Philanthropy and the Nonprofit Sector
> 810 Seventh Avenue
> New York, NY 10019
> Phone: 212-377-2700, ext. 453; fax: 212-377-2727
> Email: phil-np@ssrc.org
> Web: www.ssrc.org

Deadline and Notification: December 1 for application submission; award announcement at end of April.

Number of Awards: 7 per competition.

Award Amount: $18,000 for dissertation research; $5,000 by separate application for dissertation writing.

Application Form: Online or from the above addresses.

Purpose of Grant/Fellowship and Restrictions: To support and foster a community of social science and humanities researchers who are interested in issues in philanthropy and the nonprofit sector, including altruistic behavior, motivation, social impact, public policy, political economy, industrial structure, organizational demography, and the history of institutions. The award also includes SSRC-sponsored workshops in order to facilitate interdisciplinary dialogue and support.

Length of Award: Nine to twelve months.

Applicant Eligibility: Full-time enrollment in a doctoral program in the United States in social sciences or humanities. Women and persons of color are especially encouraged to apply.

Application Requirements: Ten copies of a completed application which includes: proposal and bibliography (limit 12 pages); autobiographical essay; three recommendations; academic transcripts.

Application Comments and Advice: SSRC is seeking clearly written proposals that demonstrate a strong academic background, particularly in theory and method. Of concern is the feasibility of the research as well as the impact it will have on the study of philanthropy and non-profits. SSRC is also looking for people who are strongly interested in networking across interdisciplinary lines now and in the future.

D. SSRC Sexuality Research Fellowship Program

Administrative Agency: Social Science Research Council

Address: SSRC

        Sexuality Research Fellowship Program

        810 Seventh Avenue

        New York, NY 10019

        Phone: 212-377-2700; fax: 212-377-2727

        Email: srfp@ssrc.org

        Web: www.ssrc.org

Deadline and Notification: Mid-December for application submission; award announcement in March.

Number of Awards: 10 dissertation, 5 postdocs, per competition.

Average Number of Applications: 60 for dissertation, 20–30 for postdocs, per competition.

Award Amount: $28,000.

Application Form: Online or from the above addresses.

Purpose of Grant/Fellowship and Restrictions: To support dissertation research in a wide range of fields that contribute "to a more thorough

understanding of human sexuality by encouraging researchers to for-
mulate new research questions, generate new theories, and apply new
methods."

Topics of special interest include: sexual/gender role socialization;
social construction analyses of sexuality; diversity/distribution of
sexual values, beliefs, and behaviors; link between sexuality and gender relations; sexual orientation; impact of institutional change (for
example, religion) on sexuality; and formation of social policy based
on cultural norms regarding sexuality.

Length of Award: One year.

Applicant Eligibility: Research conducted in the United States. Women and
minorities are encouraged to apply.

Application Requirements: Application must be done with a research advisor or associate who will act as mentor (an allowance is provided).
Completed application, which includes: research abstract; research
plan; completed research/advisor section; and department chair statement of commitment.

Application Comments and Advice: Review the application and be sure you
have a committed faculty member who will oversee the project. It is
important that the department chair is also interested enough in the
project to give it her or his full support. This is a collaborative award
that requires a faculty member's attention and involvement. Be sure
the project is appealing to the SSRC before going through the application process.

9. Woodrow Wilson Foundation Dissertation Grants in Women's Studies, and Women's and Children's Health

(Based on 2002–2003 Fellowships)

Administrative Agency: Woodrow Wilson National Fellowship Foundation

Address: Woodrow Wilson National Fellowship Foundation

    Dept. CN 5281

    Princeton, NJ 08543-5281

    Phone: 609-452-7007; fax: 609-452-0066

    Email: charlotte@woodrow.org

    Web: www.woodrow.org

Deadline and Notification: Late October for application submission; award
announcement in February.

Number of Awards: 15 for women's studies; 15 for women's and children's
health, per competition.

Average Number of Applications: 200–250 per competition.

Award Amount: $3,000.

Application Form: Online or from the email address above.

Purpose of Grant/Fellowship and Restrictions:

Women's Studies: To support research about women that crosses disciplinary, regional, or cultural boundaries. For example, topics funded include "African American Women in Electoral Politics" and "Changing Concepts of Marriage, Labor, and Culture in Southeastern China." The dissertation topic must be original and significant.

Women's and Children's Health: These two areas can be joined, as in topics like "maternal and child health development" or can be treated separately as in "predictors of childhood injuries" or "smoking, estrogen, and lung cancer." The idea is to support significant and original research. Doctoral students at the dissertation level in nursing, public health, anthropology, history, sociology, and social work are most likely to be supported.

Length of Award: One year. The dissertation is expected to be completed the summer after the award begins.

Applicant Eligibility: Doctoral students in U.S. schools who have reached candidacy around application deadline time.

Application Requirements: Completed application which includes: dissertation proposal; transcripts; expected completion date of the dissertation; name and address of dissertation director; name of another faculty reference; list of women's studies courses taught and taken.

Application Comments and Advice: Since the emphasis is on women it is important to have been involved in women's issues through course work, research, or volunteer experience.

Chapter 7
Postdoctoral Opportunities

Mary Morris Heiberger and Julia Miller Vick

A postdoctoral research opportunity, often known as a "postdoc," is a short-term appointment, frequently for one or two years, usually, although not always, begun immediately upon the completion of a doctorate. The rate of compensation typically falls between the level of a graduate student stipend and the salary of an assistant professor. Many science postdoctoral appointments are for at least two years. Year-long opportunities are most commonly found in the social sciences and humanities. In some fields, such as the biomedical sciences, such an appointment may be virtually required for a research career. In others, it may be a backup should you not receive an academic position, or provide a nice opportunity to shift research direction.

Postdoctoral opportunities fall into two broad categories. Some are in ongoing, often endowed, programs that a candidate must identify and apply for through a formal, often highly competitive process. Many of these opportunities are available through large government agencies, foundations, or research centers at universities, and they can be identified through standard directory and Internet resources. They most commonly require the candidate to propose a research project, and the funding will be awarded in terms of that specific research proposal. Of these institutional opportunities, some are "portable," meaning that the funding can be taken anywhere, and others require resident research at a particular institution.

Other opportunities, frequently in but not limited to the sciences, are more ad hoc and temporary. They are created by an established researcher's grant money and support work on a project already proposed and funded by the researcher. These opportunities are identified by seeking out researchers. Hiring, while it may be highly competitive in terms of selectivity, may be as informal a procedure as a phone call to a researcher followed by a letter, c.v., and a highly enthusiastic recommendation from one's advisor. By definition, all of these latter opportunities require work in the senior researcher's location.

This chapter will discuss the reasons for doing a postdoc; suggest ways to identify and successfully apply for opportunities; give some criteria for evaluating them; and address some specific considerations and opportunities in the sciences and in the social sciences and humanities.

General Information

There are many reasons for doing postdoctoral work. Such positions can help new Ph.D.s branch out from the focus of their dissertation work. By widening your area of expertise, you can become a more desirable candidate when going on the job market seeking a tenure-track position. If you are perceived as stuck in a very narrowly defined specialty, a department may have no interest in hiring you. However, if your work is more broadly based, you may be perceived as one who will fill both a research and teaching gap in that department.

If you are one of those unfortunate people who learned too late that someone else was also doing basically the same dissertation that you were doing, a postdoc can offer you the opportunity to redefine your research so that it is quite different from that of other scholars.

If the job market is terrible, doing a postdoc allows you to "buy time" by remaining in research. Although you are not in a tenure-track position, you have the opportunity to think about your course as a scholar, develop new mentoring relationships, get to know more people in the field, and apply for jobs. Furthermore, since tenure decisions are often heavily based on a candidate's research record, the research you do during a postdoc, without teaching obligations, will help you build the total amount of research you have to show when it comes time to be evaluated for tenure.

In science, postdocs are usually a prerequisite for research-oriented academic positions. Most research-intensive universities, and many small colleges, will not even consider a candidate for assistant or associate professor without a couple of years of postdoctoral experience. In some industries, such as the pharmaceutical industry, postdocs are also virtually required for research positions.

In the social sciences and humanities postdocs are often done out of necessity, or to build a stronger research record for the academic job market. However, more Ph.D. students are looking at them as an opportunity to enhance their research abilities and deepen their research area before going on the academic job market.

General Application Advice

Begin your search for a postdoc early, at least two years before you complete your degree. It will take time to identify and research opportunities and submit applications. Some programs will have application deadlines close to a year in advance of the time the position begins. Therefore, even if a postdoc is your second choice, you need to plan to pursue it simultaneously with your academic job search.

Use all means possible to identify opportunities. The most important place to begin the exploration is with your advisor. If you are in the sciences, where postdocs tend to be de rigueur for research careers, your advisor may regularly refer graduates to good postdoctoral opportunities in colleagues' labs. As will be discussed later, this can be a mixed blessing, especially if your research interests are beginning to diverge from your advisor's. In any case, your advisor's contacts, recommendations, and support will be important to you, so you will want to take seriously what he or she has to say. Advisors and other faculty members in your department will often be aware of additional programs and opportunities for which prior students have successfully competed.

Then move on to using all the print and Internet resources mentioned in Resources at the end of Chapter 2. Inquire everywhere you can think of. In many fields, for example, scholars who participate in listservs will respond to each other's inquiries as to what organizations may be interested in funding a particular type of research. Many scholarly associations have funding menus on their sites.

In addition to staying alert for formally announced opportunities, you should consider making inquiries with researchers with whom you wish to work or with institutions with which you would like to be affiliated. In the sciences, where externally funded research is the norm, identify the researchers whose work excites you, learn as much as you can about their work through their publications, and then contact them directly to express your interest.

In some cases, you may prefer to have a faculty member who knows the researcher make an advance phone call on your behalf. It is completely appropriate, however, for you to send a copy of your curriculum vitae, with a letter expressing your interest, directly to the researcher, and to follow this up with a phone call. If you easily establish rapport with people by phone, you may actually prefer to call first to explore the availability of options, and then follow up with a letter, curriculum vitae, and possibly reprints of publications. If you actively attend professional meetings, as you should, you can easily have informal face-to-face discussions with researchers. At the University of Pennsylvania, where our survey of new Ph.D.s asks how they obtained their positions, a frequent answer is, "I contacted researchers whose work interested me."

The same approach to a researcher that would be effective in the sciences would also be appropriate in the less common situations in the social sciences and humanities, where there are large sponsored research grants. In some cases, however, you may want to approach a researcher more as a point of contact with his or her institution, rather than as a direct source of funding.

If you would like the opportunity to be at the same institution as a senior researcher whose work you admire, you may contact that individual, whether or not he or she has external funding that could support you, to explore whether there might be some way to be affiliated with his or her institution. In many cases, this approach might merely lead to a one- or two-year teaching appointment, which would not be a postdoctoral research grant, but, occasionally, it could lead to the creation of an institutional postdoc, of which you might be the recipient.

If you are a foreign national, you may be frustrated to learn that many U.S.-based postdoctoral research opportunities require U.S. citizenship. Expand your base of opportunities by researching sources of funding in your home country, as well.

Even though you may identify opportunities informally, you will almost surely have to make formal application for them. At a minimum, you will always need to submit a curriculum vitae, letters of recommendation, and some form of written discussion of your interests. For a position with a single researcher, your written discussion may be no more than a cover letter. For direct application to an external funding agency, your written discussion might be an elaborate research proposal.

The Curriculum Vitae

A curriculum vitae, vita, or "c.v." (the terms are interchangeable) is the document that summarizes your qualifications. The construction of a curriculum vitae is beyond the scope of this chapter. However, we do stress that yours should be clear, error-free, and visually appealing. It should also be constructed in such a way that the material of most probable interest to the person or committee who will be reading it is the most visually prominent part of the curriculum vitae. Do not content yourself with looking at a fellow student's and modeling yours after it. Consult professional sources, such as your scholarly association, for materials on curriculum vitae preparation. *The Academic Job Search Handbook* (third edition, University of Pennsylvania Press, 2001) gives an extensive discussion and examples from many disciplines.

Recommendations

Recommendations have already been discussed in Chapter 2, so there is little to add here. However, if you are submitting a proposal to do a specific piece of research, it will be important to ask recommenders to discuss the importance and promise of the research itself in addition to your strengths as a candidate.

Other Written Materials

If the application procedure is merely to write a cover letter to a senior researcher, you can succinctly describe your own interests, your interests in the researcher's work, and what you can particularly contribute to his or her laboratory, such as knowledge of particular techniques or ability to develop equipment. If a full-scale research proposal is required, your ideas will have to be more specific and fleshed out in greater detail. Everything that has been discussed in terms of applying for dissertation support (see Chapter 6) is relevant in writing a proposal for postdoctoral support. You may be asked to submit all of your written materials, including your c.v., electronically.

The standards now are even higher than for graduate fellowships. By the time you receive postdoctoral funding, you have completed a Ph.D. and received your calling card into the international community of scholars. Particularly in the social sciences and humanities, you are no longer expected to be an apprentice. Instead, you are expected to be a contributor. A postdoctoral researcher in these areas is far less likely to be funded to do something for the main purpose of strengthening his or her own skill and knowledge base. It will also be more important than ever to be clear about how the short-term proposal fits into longer-term research goals, how much you can realistically expect to complete during the term of the postdoctoral grant, and, in some cases, how you would pursue additional sources of funding to continue your work. With limited funds available, funding agencies would prefer to think that they are making a long-term investment in scholars who will be productive far into the future.

Evaluating Opportunities

The whole process of pursuing postdoctoral research opportunities should involve some evaluation on your part. Why waste time preparing an application for something you do not want? Nevertheless, it's wise to apply broadly enough to be sure of obtaining something, and you may well end up with more than one opportunity from which to choose. In making a decision, you may have some personal considerations, such as salary and geographic location, which are simply a matter of your own priorities.

In professional terms, however, there are several things everyone should consider. Probably the most important question is with whom you will work. While this question weighs in most heavily when working on another researcher's grant, it is important even if you are being funded to do your own work. The researchers available to you as you pursue your research will probably have a significant intellectual impact on the outcome of your work. On a personal level, they can make a typical workday a pleasant source of challenge or a nightmare. They may also serve as important sources of recommendations and leads as you pursue a more permanent position, as well as publishing and funding opportunities. So you need to consider your own view of the quality of their work, their reputations in the field, and whatever personal characteristics they bring to the workplace.

When you choose a supervisor (which is what you are doing, even as the supervisor chooses you), consider the person's track record in working with and supporting postdocs. A good way to do this is to speak directly with some of the researcher's current or recent postdoctoral associates. To some extent you can evaluate this for yourself by using standard library sources to examine the supervisor's publications and the publications of postdocs who have worked with him or her. You can also ask the person directly to tell you about the career paths of recent postdocs. It is also important, however, to find out, through informal conversation with people in the field, what the person will be like to work with. This latter process will be useful, not only in deciding whether you want to accept the position, but also in getting off to a good start in it if you do accept it.

While you can sometimes be offered a postdoc and assess it without visiting the actual place of work, it's important to do everything within your power to visit the place so you can meet with people face-to-face. You are much more likely to form a realistic assessment of a place if you've visited it in person.

An additional consideration for foreign nationals may occasionally be whether a postdoc is with someone who will sponsor you for U.S. permanent residency. Having a "green card" is a tremendous advantage when you go on the job market, so you might want to look particularly carefully at any offer which includes this option.

The Bottom Line

A postdoctoral experience is virtually worthless unless it results in significant publications that will help you reach the next stage of your career.

You must be far more proactive in identifying, applying for, and evaluating opportunities than you probably were when you applied to your doctoral program. If you must develop your own research proposal for a postdoctoral application, think it through very carefully to make sure that it's both important and doable. If you start to run into dead ends early in your research, consider reframing it. If you will work as a postdoc on someone else's research (typically in the sciences), and arrive at the research facility only to find out that it's not at all what you expected it to be and that the odds of your success are low there, seriously consider cutting your losses and finding a more suitable appointment. Don't waste these important years at the beginning of your research career in blind alleys.

Specific Postdoctoral Opportunities

The following sampling of postdoctoral opportunities is not intended as a comprehensive list, but as an indication of what such funding opportunities look like. This listing is divided into opportunities in the sciences and engineering, opportunities in the social sciences and humanities, and opportunities available across disciplines.

Specific Postdoctoral Opportunities in the Sciences and Engineering

Scientific postdocs are particularly likely to be funded by a senior researcher, whose grant allows him or her to hire postdoctoral researchers. A very common mechanism for linking candidate and positions is through an informal word of mouth system by which an advisor calls a colleague on behalf of a student, strongly recommending the individual for a postdoctoral position. This system has certain advantages and disadvantages for candidates.

If you are lucky enough to have a good relationship with your advisor, who has a network of colleagues of national or international stature, and you are interested in continuing in the research direction of your advisor and/or the colleagues to whom he or she can recommend you, this personal referral system makes it easy to find a position. The only negative aspect of the system is that you will defer to a later stage of your career the valuable skills you learn when you first have to find your own position.

In a variation of this system, you merely continue with your current advisor as a postdoctoral appointee after the completion of your doctoral degree. You may choose this option if you are midway through an important research project that is likely to continue to yield substantial results and you want to continue working on it, or if your advisor is about to undertake some exciting new research with which you want to be associated. The potentially negative aspect of this option is that it reinforces your dependence upon one individual and deprives you of the chance to widen your circle of mentors.

If you will not be working with your advisor, and he or she does not recommend you to close associates with whom you would like to work, or if you want to shift research direction, you will not want to limit yourself to the contacts provided by your advisor and should search more pro-actively on your own, as described above.

Industrial postdoctoral positions are another option, most common in the chemical and pharmaceutical industries. While these can provide valuable industry experience, you must generally keep in mind that they are postdoctoral rather than career-track research and development positions. Do not assume that an industrial postdoc represents a "foot in the door" of the company, unless there is internal evidence that is in fact the case. Commonly companies make a practice of not hiring their own postdocs. Therefore it may not be wise to accept a postdoctoral position at a company that is your first choice for subsequent permanent employment.

Most funding for scientific postdocs comes from the U.S. government. The primary sources are the National Science Foundation (primarily, although not exclusively, for the physical sciences), the National Institutes of Health (for the biomedical sciences), and national research laboratories such as Oak Ridge. Other civilian agencies, such as the Departments of Agriculture and Energy, offer postdocs, as do military agencies. Many of these are funneled through the Research Associateships Program of the National Research Council.

Direct U.S. funding often requires U.S. permanent residency, and sometimes citizenship. Foreign nationals who are not U.S. permanent residents may receive finding as postdocs on another individual's research grant, because in that case funding is channeled through the researcher's institution. See the online Community of Science, www.cos.com, and GrantsNet, www.grantsnet.org, for free searchable databases of grants.

The conditions under which postdocs work, particularly in the biomedical sciences, has been a subject of national debate. See *Enhancing the Postdoctoral Experience for Scientists and Engineers: A Guide for Postdoctoral Scholars, Advisers, Institutions, Funding Organizations, and Disciplinary Societies*, compiled by the National Academy of Sciences, National Academy of Engineering, Institute of Medicine (National Academy Press, 2000). One recent initiative to help postdocs share information is the Postdoc Network, a free listserv and site at http://nextwave.sciencemag.org/

feature/postdocnetwork.shtml. Also, Science's Next Wave, an online journal for scientists at the early stages of their careers, offers valuable information. See www.nextwave.org. There is a subscription fee for full NextWave access, but check to see whether your institution has taken out an institutional subscription you can use at no additional charge.

1. National Science Foundation Postdoctoral Programs

NSF is a major source of science postdoctoral funding. It sponsors twelve postdoctoral fellowship programs. For further information on each listed below, contact the appropriate office and division.

Administrative Office: National Science Foundation
Address: 4201 Wilson Boulevard
       Arlington, VA 22230
       Phone: 703-292-5111 FIRS: 800-877-8339 TDD: 703-292-5090
       Email: info@nsf.gov
       Web: www.nsf.gov
Eligibility: With the exception of the NSF-NATO Postdoctoral Research Fellowships listed below, eligibility is limited to U.S. citizens and permanent residents.

A. Astronomy and Astrophysics Postdoctoral Fellowships (AAPF)
Administrative Agency: Division of Astronomical Sciences
Web: www.nsf.gov/cgi-bin/getpub?nsf00136

B. Postdoctoral Research Fellowships in Biological Informatics
Administrative Agency: Directorate for Biological Sciences
Web: www.nsf.gov/cgi-bin/getpub?nsf98162

C. CISE Postdoctoral Research Associates in Experimental Computer Science
Administrative Office: Directorate for Computer and Information Science and Engineering
Web: www.nsf.gov/cgi-bin/getpub?nsf97169

D. MPS Distinguished International Postdoctoral Research Fellowships (MPS-DRF)
Administrative Office: Directorate for Mathematical and Physical Sciences
Web: www.nsf.gov/cgi-bin/getpub?nsf00142

E. Mathematical Sciences Postdoctoral Research Fellowships
Administrative Agency: Division of Mathematical Sciences
Web: www.nsf.gov/cgi-bin/getpub?nsf98135

F. Minority Postdoctoral Research Fellowships and Supporting Activities
Web: www.nsf.gov/cgi-bin/getpub?nsf00139
Administrative Offices: Directorate for Biological Sciences; Division of Biological Infrastructure; Directorate for Social, Behavioral, and Economic Sciences; Division of Behavioral and Cognitive Sciences; Division of Social and Economic Sciences

G. NSF-NATO Postdoctoral Fellowships in Science and Engineering Including Special Fellowship Opportunities for Scientists from NATO Partner Countries
Administrative Office: Division of Graduate Education; Directorate for Education and Human Resources
Web: www.nsf.gov/cgi-bin/getpub?nsf00145
Eligibility: U.S. citizens and permanent residents and citizens of NATO partner countries nominated by U.S. institutions.

H. Postdoctoral Research Fellowships in Microbial Biology
Administrative Agency: Directorate for Biological Sciences, Division of Biological Infrastructure
Web: www.nsf.gov/cgi-bin/getpub?nsf99142

I. Postdoctoral Fellowships in Science, Mathematics, Engineering and Technology Education (PFSMETE)
Administrative Agency: Directorate for Education and Human Resources, Division of Graduate Education
Web: www.nsf.gov/cgi-bin/getpub?nsf9917

2. National Research Service Award Individual Postdoctoral Fellowships (F32)

Administrative Agency: National Institutes of Health
Address: Division of Extramural Outreach and Information Resources
Office of Extramural Research
National Institutes of Health
Two Rockledge Center, Room 6095
6701 Rockledge Drive, MSC 7910
Bethesda, MD 20892-7910
Phone: 301-435-0714; fax: 301-480-0525
Email: grantsinfo@nih.gov
Web: http://grants.nih.gov/training/careerdev/pdfopporte.
html#nationalresearchf32
Deadline and Notification: Applications are due April 5, August 5, and December 5. Results are announced in January, May, and September.

There is no fixed start date, but awards must be activated within six months unless an extension has been approved by the awarding unit.

Number of Awards: There were 868 awards in 1999–2000.

Average Number of Applicants: There were 1,910 applicants in 1999–2000.

Award Amount: $26,916–$42,300 per year for salary plus $4,000 per year for training-related expenses. There are salary increments for additional years of experience. As of 2001, there was discussion of raising this amount substantially. Requires one month of payback for each month of training, up to a maximum of twelve months. This requirement can be fulfilled by teaching or research (a minimum of twenty hours per week) on a continuous basis, beginning within two years after support ends.

Application Form: Available from institutional offices of sponsored research or from http//grants.nih.gov/grants/funding/416/phs416.htm.

Purpose of Grant/Fellowship and Restrictions: This award offers health scientists the opportunity to receive full-time research training in areas that reflect the national need for biomedical and behavioral research and is offered by all the NIH institutes and centers.

Length of Award: Full-time for up to three years.

Applicant Eligibility: When the fellowship begins, the applicant must have received a doctoral degree and have arranged to work with a sponsor affiliated with an institution that has the staff and facilities needed for the proposed training. Applicants must be U.S. citizens, noncitizen nationals, or legal permanent residents of the United States. Training can be conducted abroad if the site provides opportunities that are not available in the United States.

Application Requirements: You and the institution which will sponsor you must each submit an extremely detailed application, giving extensive information about both your background and your proposed research. In addition, you need to submit three letters of recommendation.

Application Advice: Because the application is so detailed and time-consuming, and requires the cooperation of other people, get the application early, read it carefully, and allow yourself plenty of time to meet all the requirements. In addition, the NIH offers other awards.

A. *Medical Informatics Research Training*
Candidates may apply for individually mentored research.
Web: http://grants.nih.gov/training/careerdev/pdfopporte.html#medicalinforesearch

B. *Mentored Research Scientist Development Award*
Provides an additional period of support in an area new to the candidate to enhance the candidate's scientific career.

Web: http://grants.nih.gov/training/careerdev/pdfopporte.html#
mentoredresearchk01

C. NCI Mentored Career Development Award
Career development support for research or health professional doctorate who previously had support from an NCI minority supplement
award.
Web: http://grants.nih.gov/training/careerdev/pdfopporte.html#
ncimentoredk01

D. Research Supplements for Underrepresented Minority Individuals in
Postdoctoral Training
Web: http://grants.nih.gov/training/careerdev/pdfopporte.html#
researchsuppunder

E. Research Supplements to Promote the Recruitment of Individuals with
Disabilities into Biomedical Research Careers
Web: http://grants.nih.gov/training/careerdev/pdfopporte.html#
researchsupppromote

F. Supplements to Promote Reentry into Biomedical and Behavioral Research
Careers
Web: http://grants.nih.gov/training/careerdev/pdfopporte.html#
supplementsbio

3. AAAS Science and Engineering Fellowship Program

Administrative Agency: American Association for the Advancement of
Science
Address: Directorate for Science and Policy Programs
      1333 H Street, NW
      Washington, DC 20005
      Phone: 202-326-6600; fax: 202-289-4950
      Email: science_policy@aaas.org
      Web: www.aaas.org/careers/fellowships.html
Deadline: January 10. Interviews are held with finalists in March.
Number of Awards: Overall, AAAS awards about fifty fellowships each year.
In addition, approximately thirty Congressional Fellows are selected
by other national science and engineering societies.
Average Number of Applicants: Awards are highly competitive. Ratio of appli-
cants to awardees varies by program.
Award Amount: $52,000.
Application Form: Available online.

Purpose of Grant/Fellowship and Restrictions: To provide opportunities for scientists and engineers to work on public policy issues in Congress and several other executive branch agencies.

Length of Award: One year.

Applicant Eligibility: For all of these, candidates must be U.S. citizens. Applicants must have a Ph.D. or equivalent doctoral-level degree at the time of application.

Application Requirements: Cover letter, letter of intent, c.v., candidate statement, certification of accuracy and citizenship, three letters of recommendation. Interviews are held with finalists in March.

Application Advice: The ratio of applicants to fellowships awarded is different in each of the AAAS programs. The AAAS urges you not to consider "the odds," but to apply to the programs that best fit your areas of experience and interest, because it is in those areas that you will be most competitive. Read through the program descriptions carefully. If you belong to one of the thirty professional societies which sponsor Congressional Fellows, you may apply through it as well as for a fellowship whose awardees are selected by AAAS.

AAAS Congressional Fellowships
Web: http://fellowships.aaas.org/congressional/index.html

AAAS Roger Revelle Fellowship in Global Stewardship
Web: http://fellowships.aaas.org/revelle/index.html

AAAS/NSF Fellowship Program
Web: http://fellowships.aaas.org/research/index.html

AAAS Diplomacy Fellowships
Web: http://fellowships.aaas.org/diplomacy/index.html

AAAS Risk Policy Fellowships
Web: http://fellowships.aaas.org/risk/index.html

AAAS Defense Policy Fellowships
Web: http://fellowships.aaas.org/defense/index.html

AAAS/EPA Environmental Fellowships
Web: http://fellowships.aaas.org/environmental/index.html

AAAS/NIH Science Policy Fellowships
Web: http://fellowships.aaas.org/nih/index.html

Science, Justice, and Public Policy Fellowships
Web: http://fellowships.aaas.org/doj/index.html

4. Helen Hay Whitney Foundation Postdoctoral Research Fellowships

Administrative Agency: Helen Hay Whitney Foundation
Address: 450 East 63rd Street
New York, NY 10021
Phone: 212-751-8228
Email: hhws@earthlink.net
Web: www.hhwf.org/HTMLSrc/ResearchFellowships.html
Deadline and Notification: August 15 for activation July 1 of the following year. Notification in January.
Number of Awards: 22 per competition.
Average Number of Applicants: 325 per competition.
Other Related Fellowships: Irvington Institute for Immunological Research, Damon Runyon-Walter Winchell Cancer Research Fund, Jane Coffin Childs Memorial Fund, NRSAs from NIH.
Award Amount: As of 2001, first-year stipend was $36,000; second year, $39,000; third year, $42,000, with a $2,000 research allowance in each of the three years. Travel allowance to the research site.
Application Form: The application is available online.
Purpose of Fellowship and Restrictions: To increase the number of imaginative, well-trained, and dedicated medical scientists. The foundation does not make more than one award in any one year for training with a given supervisor, and in addition, will not support more than two fellows per laboratory at one time.
Length of Award: Three years.
Applicant Eligibility: Candidates living in North America who hold, or are in the final stages of obtaining, the M.D., Ph.D., or equivalent degree and are seeking beginning postdoctoral training in basic biomedical research. Applicants must meet the first August deadline after completion of their degree. U.S. citizenship is not a requirement, but fellowships to resident noncitizens are awarded for training only in the United States. U.S. citizens may train abroad.
Application Requirements: Application form, summary of prior research accomplishments, bibliography, autobiographical sketch, research proposal, statement of general and specific professionals interests, goals for the fellowship period, long-range career objectives, transcripts, reprints, letter from prospective supervisor, and four letters of reference.

5. Jane Coffin Childs Memorial Fund for Medical Research Fellowship

Administrative Agency: Jane Coffin Childs Memorial Fund for Medical
  Research
Address: 333 Cedar Street
            New Haven, CT 06510
            Phone: 203-785-4612
            Email: info@jccfund.org
            Web: www.jccfund.org/
Deadline: February 1.
Number of Awards: 25–30 per competition.
Average Number of Applicants: 250–300 per competition.
Other Related Fellowships: Irvington Institute for Immunological Research,
  Damon Runyon-Walter Winchell Cancer Research Fund, NRSAs from
  NIH, Helen Hay Whitney Foundation.
Award Amount: $33,500 the first year; $35,000 the second year; $37,000
  the third year, with an additional $750 for each dependent child. An
  allowance of $1,500 a year toward the cost of the research usually will
  be made available to the laboratory sponsoring the fellow. A travel
  award will be made to the fellow and family for travel to the sponsoring laboratory.
Application Form: Application request form is available online.
Purpose of Grant/Fellowship and Restrictions: The fund awards fellowships to
  suitably qualified individuals for full-time postdoctoral studies in the
  medical and related sciences bearing on cancer. Applicants in general
  should not have more than one year of postdoctoral experience.
Length of Award: Normally three years. Applicants who have completed a
  year of postdoctoral research by the time the fellowship begins will
  normally be awarded two years of support.
Applicant Eligibility: Applicants should hold an M.D. or Ph.D. degree in the
  field in which they propose to study. Applications will also be accepted
  in the field of structural biology and will emphasize supramolecular
  structure and cryoelectron microscopy. Citizens of any country are eligible, but awards to foreign nationals will be made only for U.S. study.
Application Requirements: Evidence of pre- and postdoctoral training,
  three references (one of whom should be the principal predoctoral
  advisor), outline of the research problem proposed, and the written
  consent of the chief of laboratory and a responsible fiscal officer of
  the host institution.
Application Advice: Focus on developing a sound research proposal which
  has the support of the laboratory where you want to work and which
  can be executed with its facilities.

6. NRC Research Associateship Program

Administrative Agency: National Research Council
Address: Associateship Programs—TJ 2114
　　　　National Research Council
　　　　2001 Wisconsin Avenue, NW
　　　　Washington, DC 20007
　　　　Phone: 202-334-2760; fax: 202-334-2759
　　　　Email: rap@nas.edu
　　　　Web: www4.nationalacademies.org/pga/rap.nsf
Deadline: January 15 for February review; April 15 for June review; August 15 for October review. Not all laboratories participate in all review sessions, so check with the laboratory to which you wish to apply.
Number of Awards: 350 in 2000.
Average Number of Applicants: 750–1,200. There were 800 in 2000.
Award Amount: Varies by agency, with typical amounts ranging from the upper $30,000s to mid-$50,000s.
Application form: Available online.
Purpose of Grant/Fellowship and Restrictions: The NRC Research Associate-ship Programs are awards made to doctorate-level scientists and engineers who can bring their special knowledge and research talents to work in research areas of interest to them, to the host laboratories, and to the research centers. Postdoctoral awards are made to those who have earned their doctorates within the last five years. Each awardee works in collaboration with a research advisor, who is a staff member of the laboratory.

　　NRC administers the program for thirty-five federal laboratories and NASA Research. Centers at over one hundred locations in the United States and overseas include:
　　Aerospace Corporation (AERO)
　　Air Force Research Laboratory (AFRL)
　　Air Force Summer Faculty Fellowship Program (AF/SFFP)
　　Albany Research Center (ALRC)
　　Armed Forces Radiobiology Research Institute (AFRRI)
　　Center for Devices and Radiological Health (CDRH)
　　Federal Highway Administration/Turner-Fairbank Highway
　　NASA Ames Research Center (ARC)
　　NASA Astrobiology Institute (NAI)
　　NASA Dryden Flight Research Center (DFRC)
　　NASA George C. Marshall Space Flight Center (MSFC)
　　NASA Goddard Space Flight Center (GSFC)
　　NASA Jet Propulsion Laboratory (JPL)

NASA John C. Stennis Space Center (SSC)

NASA John F. Kennedy Space Center (KSC)

NASA John H. Glenn Research Center at Lewis Field (GRC)

NASA Langley Research Center (LARC)

NASA Lyndon B. Johnson Space Center (JSC)

National Energy Technology Laboratory (NETL)

National Institute for Occupational Safety and Health

National Institute of Standards and Technology (NIST)

National Institutes of Health (NIH)

National Oceanic and Atmospheric Administration (NOAA)

Naval Medical Research Center/Naval Health Research Center

Naval Postgraduate School (NPS)

Naval Research Laboratory (NRL)

Space and Naval Warfare Systems Center (SPAWARSYSCEN)

U.S. Army Aviation and Missile Command (AMCOM)

U.S. Army CECOM-Night Vision and Electronic Sensors Directorate (CECOM/NVESD)

U.S. Army Edgewood Chemical and Biological Center—U.S. Army Soldier and Biological Chemical Command (ECBC)

U.S. Army Medical Research and Materiel Command (AMRMC)

U.S. Army Natick Soldier Center—U.S. Army Soldier and Biological Chemical Command (ECBC)

U.S. Army Research Laboratory (ARL)

U.S. Army Research Office (ARO)

U.S. Army TACOM Armament Research Development and Engineering Center (TACOM/ARDEC)

U.S. Environmental Protection Agency (EPA)

U.S. Geological Survey (USGS)

U.S. Military Academy/U.S. Army Research Laboratory (USMA/ARL)

Length of Award: Tenure varies by agency, but an initial appointment of one year is typical.

Applicant Eligibility: Some of these awards require U.S. citizenship, and some do not. Foreign nationals can search the web site to find associateships for which they are eligible.

Application Requirements: Application form, research proposal and appendix, description of previous and current research, transcripts, reference reports or letters of reference, signed checklist.

Application Advice: It is essential to search the web site carefully to find opportunities that correspond to your research interest. After you have identified an appropriate opportunity, you will need to contact the relevant research advisor to explore how your plans will mesh with ongoing research. Since you will be evaluated on your proposal as well as on your background, it is essential to propose research that is well thought-out and that will receive the research advisor's strong support.

Specific Postdoctoral Opportunities in the Social Sciences and Humanities

Because fewer researchers in most disciplines in these areas receive grants large enough to support postdoctoral researchers, most funding will be available through direct application to external funding agencies. An occasional exception, discussed above, is the opportunity to work with some very senior researcher. Since more postdocs are beginning to be created in these fields, it is particularly important to stay in touch with opportunities. Follow announcements in the *Chronicle of Higher Education* and in all the scholarly job listings that could possibly apply to your research. If *ARIS* or *The Grants Advisor* are available on your campus or at a library near you, watch their current issues. If you subscribe to any listservs, note announcements of postdoctoral opportunities. Continue to ask everyone who might know, in your department, at meetings, via phone calls and email messages. Many research centers, including major libraries and museums, have some funding for those wishing to work there or to use their collections. Make sure to contact them directly to see if you can identify additional funding.

Below are listed some of the major sources of external funding for which candidates in the humanities and social sciences may apply directly. Use this list only as a starting point, taking care to consult the resources discussed above.

7. U.S. Fulbright Scholar Program

Administrative Agency: Council for International Exchange of Scholars
Address: 3007 Tilden Street, NW, Suite 5L
        Washington, DC 20008-3009
        Phone: 202-686-4000; fax: 202-362-3442
        Email: apprequest@cies.iie.org
        Web: www.cies.org/cies/us_scholars/
Deadline and Notification: August deadline (for an academic year starting thirteen months later).
Number of Awards: 800 awards in 140 countries. One-fifth are for research and four-fifths are for lecturing, combined lecturing and research, or seminar participation.

Average Number of Applicants: Ranges from 2,500 to 3,000 per year.

Award Amount: Varies and includes a base stipend, maintenance for living in country of assignment, travel and relocation, and health insurance.

Application Form: Available on the web site.

Purpose of Grant/Fellowship and Restrictions: The Fulbright Scholar Program is sponsored by the U.S. Department of State, Bureau of Educational and Cultural Affairs. It offers grants for college and university faculty as well as for professionals and independent scholars to lecture and conduct research in countries around the world.

Length of Award: Academic year, which can vary according to country.

Applicant Eligibility: U.S. faculty and professionals who are U.S. citizens. Applicants must have a Ph.D. or equivalent professional/terminal degree at time of application. They must also have college or university teaching experience at the level and in the field of the proposed lecturing activity as specified in the award description and foreign language proficiency if specified in the award description.

Application Requirements: All application materials must be submitted on 8½" × 11" white paper. Responses to questions on the four-page application form must fit on the pages on which the questions originally appear. For some awards, in addition to the signed application form, applicant may need to provide project statement, select bibliography, curriculum vitae or resume, sample course syllabi letter of invitation references and teaching report, language proficiency form, additional materials, and reply card.

Application Advice: The Fulbright web site has "Tips for Prospective Applicants."

8. Mellon Postdoctoral Fellowships in the Humanities

Each year a few select institutions have been funded by the Mellon Foundation to provide research opportunities in the humanities. The individual institutions determine the areas of research, which usually change each year, and advertise them in the *Chronicle of Higher Education* and appropriate scholarly journals. They are not advertised or listed as a group. Applicants from other institutions are preferred to those who earned doctorates at the institutions offering the fellowship. Most fellowships are for two years and do not involve teaching. There are approximately two to six fellowships at each institution. Sites to some institutions with Mellon postdocs are listed here: University of Pennsylvania (www.humanities.sas.upenn.edu/mellonf.htm); *Cornell University (www.arts.cornell.edu/sochum/html/index.html);* and Washington University in St. Louis www.artsci.wustl.edu/~szwicker/Mellon_Postdoctoral_Program

9. Individual Advanced Research Opportunities for U.S. Scholars in Central and Eastern Europe

Administrative Agency: International Research and Exchange Board (IREX)

Address: 2121 K Street, NW, Suite 700
Washington, DC 20037
Phone: 202-628-8188; fax: 202-628-8189
Email: irex@irex.org
Web: www.irex.org

Deadline and Notification: November 1; March 1 award notification.

Number of Awards: 37 per competition.

Average Number of Applicants: 200 per competition.

Award Amount: Round-trip airfare and visa fees. Stipend for living expenses based on academic salary at the time of application. Stipend for host-country room and board.

Application Form: The application is available on the IREX Web site.

Purpose of Grant/Fellowship and Restrictions: This program provides fellowships for individual long-term research in Central and Eastern Europe and Eurasia. Limited funding is available for cross-regional research in Turkey and Iran for postdoctoral humanities scholars. The Web site lists approved countries.

Length of Award: Two to nine months.

Applicant Eligibility: U.S. citizen or permanent resident for three years prior to submitting an application. Command of host-country language sufficient for advanced research. Applicants are required to have a full-time affiliation with a college or university and to be faculty members or doctoral candidates who will have completed all requirements for the Ph.D. except the dissertation by the time of participation. Independent scholars or recipients of professional degrees (M.F.A., J.D., M.D., M.L.I.S., M.B.A., M.P.A.) may also qualify.

Application Requirements: A transcript and letters of recommendation should be sent with the application.

Application Advice: Grants are divided into two categories: fellowships in the humanities and fellowships in policy research and development. Scholars can apply to both fields, but must demonstrate relevance to each field. Scholars in cross-disciplinary and cross-country/regional studies are strongly encouraged to apply.

10. National Academy of Education Spencer Postdoctoral Fellowship

Administrative Agency: National Academy of Education

Address: National Academy of Education
New York University
School of Education
726 Broadway, Room 509
New York, NY 10003-9580
Phone: 212-998-9035; fax: 212-995-4435
Email: nae.info@nyu.edu
Web: www.nae.nyu.edu/spencer/index.htm

Deadline and Notification: December 1 application deadline; award notification in May.

Number of Awards: Up to 30 per competition.

Average Number of Applicants: 200 per competition.

Award Amounts: $50,000 for one academic year of research, or $25,000 for each of two contiguous years, working half-time.

Application Form: Available on the web site.

Purpose of Grant/Fellowship and Restrictions: The NAE Spencer Postdoctoral Fellowships are designed to promote scholarship in the United States and abroad on matters relevant to the improvement of education in all its forms.

Length of Award: One academic year or two contiguous years, working half-time.

Applicant Eligibility: Applicants must have been awarded their Ph.D., Ed.D., or equivalent degree between the January six years prior to the deadline and December 31 of the year of the deadline. Applicants must be in education, the humanities, or the social and behavioral sciences.

Application Requirements: Applicants must describe research relevant to education. Applications will be judged on the applicant's past research record, the promise of early work, and the quality of the project described in the application.

11. Smithsonian Postdoctoral Fellowships

Administrative Agency: Smithsonian Institution

Address: Office of Fellowships and Grants
Smithsonian Institution
750 9th Street, NW, Suite 9300
Washington, DC 20560-0902
Phone: 202-275-0655
Email: siofg@ofg.si.edu
Web: www.si.edu/ofg/fell.htm

Deadline and Notification: January 15; mid-April notification.

Number of Awards: 30 per competition.

Average Number of Applicants: 160–170 per competition.

Award Amount: $27,000 for twelve months; allowances to assist with the fellow's research-related expenses and for temporary relocation to the Smithsonian are possible. Stipends are prorated for periods of less than twelve months.

Application Form: Application available on web site at www.si.edu/ofg/.

Purpose of Grant/Fellowship and Restrictions: To provide opportunities to conduct research in association with members of the Smithsonian professional research staff, and to utilize the resources of the institution. Fields of research and study are available on the web site.

Length of Award: Three to twelve months; must begin between June 1 and March 1.

Applicant Eligibility: For scholars who have held the doctoral degree or equivalent for fewer than seven years as of the application deadline.

Application Requirements: Applicants must submit detailed proposals including justification for conducting the research in residence at the Institution. Must submit an original plus multiple copies of the completed cover sheet, research proposal, curriculum vitae, transcripts, letters of reference and one completed notification card.

Application Advice: Applicants are evaluated on the scholarly merit of their proposals; their ability to carry out the proposed research and study; the likelihood that the research can be completed during the requested appointment period; extent to which the Smithsonian, through its research staff members or resources, can contribute to the proposed research project; and the inclusion of diverse perspectives.

12. Postdoctoral Fellowships and Advanced Research Grants

Administrative Agency: Social Science Research Council

Address: 810 Seventh Avenue, 31st Floor
New York, NY 10019
Phone: 212-377-2700; fax: 212-377-2727
Email: info@ssrc.org
Web: www.ssrc.org

The SSRC offers many postdoctoral programs. In 2001–2002 there were fourteen.

Deadline: Varies, check web site.

Number of Awards: Varies, check web site.

Number of Applicants: Varies, contact SSRC.

Award Amount: Varies, check web site.

Application Form: Application materials on web site.

Purpose of Grant/Fellowship and Restrictions: The Social Science Research Council is an independent, nonprofit organization that seeks to advance social science throughout the world, and supports research, education and scholarly exchange on every continent. The SSRC sponsors fellowship and grant programs, either independently or with other organizations. Some programs also provide support for natural scientists and nonacademic professionals.

SSRC administers postdoctoral programs in the following areas: Abe Fellowships; Berlin Program for Advanced German and European Studies; Cuba Grant Competition; Eastern Europe; Eurasia; European and American Young Scholars' Institutes Program; Global Security and Cooperation (GSC); Information Technology, International Cooperation, and Global Security Summer Fellowships; ACLS/SSRC/NEH International and Area Studies Fellowships; International Migration; Japan Studies; and Sexuality Research Fellowships.

Length of Award: Varies.

Application Form: Applications for some fellowships are available online. Check the web site.

Application Advice: For advice on submitting fellowship proposals to the Council, see "The Art of Writing Proposals: Some Candid Suggestions for Applicants to Social Science Research Council Competitions," by two long-time selection committee members. It is available on the web site.

13. Getty Postdoctoral Fellowships

Administrative Agency: Getty Grant Program

Address: Senior Program Officer, Research Fellowships
　　　　　Getty Grant Program
　　　　　1200 Getty Center Drive, Suite 800
　　　　　Los Angeles, CA 90049-1685
　　　　　Phone: 310-440-7374; fax: 310-440-7703
　　　　　Email: researchgrants@getty.edu
　　　　　Web: www.getty.edu/grants/

Deadline and Notification: November 1; notification in March.

Number of Awards: Approximately 15 per competition.

Average Number of Applicants: 100–150 per competition.

Amounts Awarded: $35,000.

Purpose of Grant/Fellowship and Restrictions: Support is available for outstanding scholars who are within six years of having earned their doctorate (or equivalent degree in countries outside the United States) and who demonstrate that their work has the potential to make a substantial and original contribution to the history of art. Fellows pursue their research wherever necessary to complete their projects. Although grantees are welcome to use the Getty Library if their projects bring them to Los Angeles, the fellowships are nonresidential.

Length of Award: Ten months (June–September).

Application Form: Each year's application form is available on the web site in June.

Purpose of Grant/Fellowship and Restrictions: Provide support for outstanding scholars in the early stages of their careers to pursue interpretive research projects on topics that make a substantial and original contribution to the understanding of art and its history.

Applicant Eligibility: Scholars of all nationalities whose doctoral degrees in art history (or the equivalent in countries outside the United States) have been or will be officially conferred between January six years before the application deadline and January after the deadline. Candidates who hold doctoral degrees in fields outside of art history are eligible to apply if they can demonstrate that their work promises to make a substantial and original contribution to the discipline of art history.

Application Requirements: Application form, recommendations, curriculum vitae.

Application Advice: Potential applicants should review the Getty's funding priorities before submitting a preliminary letter or an application. Application procedures and deadlines vary by grant category.

14. ACLS Fellowships

Administrative Agency: American Council of Learned Societies
Address: 228 East 45th Street
New York, NY 10017-3398
Phone: 212-697-1505
Email: grants@acls.org
Web: www.acls.org

Deadline and Notification: October; award notification in mid-March.

Number of Awards: 60 per competition.

Average Number of Applicant: 600 per competition.

Amounts Awarded: $30,000–$50,000, depending on rank.

Application form: Information on programs is posted in June. A printed descriptive brochure and application materials are also available then.

Purpose of Grant/Fellowship and Restrictions: ACLS Fellowships, including ACLS/SSRC/NEH International and Area Studies Fellowships and ACLS/New York Public Library Residential Fellowships, are for postdoctoral research in the humanities and related social sciences.

Length of Award: Six to twelve consecutive months devoted to full-time research.

Applicant Eligibility: Applicants must be citizens or permanent legal residents of the United States. Applicants must have Ph.D. conferred no later than October 1 of the year of the fellowship deadline. Established scholars who can demonstrate the equivalent of the Ph.D. in publications and professional experience may also qualify. At least three years must have passed since the applicant's last "supported research leave."

Application Requirements: Applicants must submit a detailed proposal of their research plans with their application.

Application Advice: Fellows and grantees in all programs will be selected by committees of scholars appointed for this purpose. An individual may apply to as many fellowship and grant programs as are suitable. However, not more than one ACLS or ACLS-joint award may normally be accepted in any one competition year. Younger scholars and independent scholars who do not hold academic appointments are encouraged to apply.

15. Ford Foundation Postdoctoral Fellowships for Minorities

Administrative Agency: National Research Council
Address: Fellowship Programs Office/FP, TJ 2041
　　　　　　National Research Council
　　　　　　2001 Wisconsin Avenue, NW
　　　　　　Washington, DC 20007
　　　　　　Phone: 202-334-2860; fax: 202-334-3419
　　　　　　Email: infofell@nas.edu
　　　　　　Web: www.nationalacademies.org/opportunities/
Deadline and Notification: January; award notification in April.
Number of Awards: Approximately 30 per competition.
Average Number of Applicants: 150 per competition.
Award Amount: $35,000 stipend; $3,000 travel and relocation allowance; $2,000 cost-of-research allowance; and $2,500 employing institution allowance
Application Form: An online application becomes available in August
Purpose of Grant/Fellowship and Restrictions: Program identifies outstanding researchers and scholars who are members of minority groups whose underrepresentation in the professoriate and in formal programs of postdoctoral study and research in the United States has been long-standing and remains severe as a result of past discrimination. The program enables fellows to engage in a year of postdoctoral research and scholarship in an environment free from the interference of their normal professional duties. In sponsoring this fellowship program, the Ford Foundation wishes to help recent doctoral recipients achieve greater recognition and develop the professional associations that will make them more effective and productive in

academic employment. Major disciplines eligible for support include the life sciences, physical sciences, mathematics, engineering sciences, behavioral and social sciences, education, and the humanities.

Length of Award: Either nine or twelve months, beginning in September.

Applicant Eligibility: U.S. citizens or nationals of the United States at the time of application and who are members of the following groups: Native American Indians, Alaskan Natives (Eskimo or Aleut), Black/ African Americans, Mexican Americans/Chicanas/Chicanos, Native Pacific Islanders (Micronesian or Polynesian), Puerto Ricans. Applicants are required to have earned a Ph.D. or Sc.D. degree from a U.S. educational institution no earlier than January 8 seven years prior to the fellowship year and no later than February 28 of the fellowship year in a field supported by this program. Only those already engaged in a teaching and research career or those planning such a career are eligible.

Application Requirements: Confidential information form, fellowship application form, one-page abstract of the proposed plan of study or research, host letter (endorsing the applicant's prospective affiliation with the fellowship institution), four letters of reference, transcript from the doctorate-granting institution, a working bibliography, and an annotated bibliography. See web site for complete list of materials that may be submitted.

Application Advice: Fellowship applicants are encouraged to choose a fellowship institution other than the institution with which they are affiliated at the time of application. Appropriate institutions include universities, museums, libraries, government or national laboratories, privately sponsored not-for-profit institutes, government-chartered not-for-profit research organizations, and centers for advanced study. Each applicant is expected to designate a faculty member or other scholar who will serve as host at the proposed fellowship institution. Each applicant must present a clearly articulated plan of study or research that will further his or her career in higher education. Applicants should explain fully the particular benefits that would accrue from affiliation with the proposed institution.

16. American Fellowships, Postdoctoral Research Leave Fellowships

Administrative Agency: American Association of University Women Educational Foundation

Address: AAUW Educational Foundation
1111 Sixteenth Street, NW
Washington, DC 20036

Phone: 202-728-7602; fax: 202-463-7169

Email: foundation@aauw.org

Web: www.aauw.org/7000/aboutef.html

Deadline and Notification: Mid-November postmark deadline; award notification in April.

Number of Awards: 20 per competition.

Average Number of Applicants: 100–150 per competition.

Other Related Fellowships: AAUW Educational Foundation International Fellowships (www.aauw.org/3000/fdnfelgra/internat.html) are awarded for full-time study or research at accredited institutions to women who are not U.S. citizens or permanent residents. The fellowships support graduate and postgraduate study.

Amounts Awarded: $27,000.

Application Form: Applications become available in mid-August.

Purpose of Grant/Fellowship and Restrictions: American Fellowships support women doctoral candidates completing dissertations or scholars seeking funds for postdoctoral research leave from accredited institutions. Candidates are evaluated on the basis of scholarly excellence, teaching experience, and active commitment to helping women and girls through service in their communities, professions, or fields of research. There are no restrictions on the location, field of study, or age of the applicant.

Length of Award: One year, July 1–June 30.

Applicant Eligibility: Applicants must be U.S. citizens or permanent residents and have achieved a doctorate by mid-November of the year of the deadline.

Application Requirements: A five-page proposal, narrative autobiography, a detailed c.v., and three recommendations.

Application Advice: It is important that the applicant demonstrate a commitment to helping girls and women.

17. National Humanities Center

Administrative Agency: National Humanities Center

Address: 7 Alexander Drive

PO Box 12256

Research Triangle Park, NC 27709

Phone: 919-549-0661; fax: 919-990-8535

Email: lmorgan@ga.unc.edu

Web: www.nhc.rtp.nc.us:8080

Deadline and Notification: Mid-October; award notification in mid-February.

Number of Awards: 40 per competition.

Average Number of Applicants: 400–500 per competition.

Other Related Fellowships: Institute for Advanced Study (www.ias.edu) and the Center for Advanced Study in the Visual Arts (www.nga.gov/resources/casva.htm).

Award Amount: Fellowship stipends are individually determined and depend upon the needs of the fellow and the center's ability to meet them. As the center cannot in most instances replace full salary, applicants are urged to seek partial support in the form of sabbatical salaries or grants from other sources. Round-trip travel expenses to the center are provided.

Application Form: Application form is available on the web site.

Purpose of Grant/Fellowship and Restrictions: The National Humanities Center is a residential institute for advanced study in history, languages and literature, philosophy, and other fields of the humanities. Each year the center awards fellowships to scholars of demonstrated achievement and to promising younger scholars. Fellows are expected to work at the center.

The center exists to encourage excellent scholarship and to affirm the importance of the humanities in American society. In addition to scholars from fields normally associated with the humanities, representatives of the natural and social sciences, the arts, the professions, and public life may be awarded fellowships if their work has humanistic dimensions.

Length of Award: Most fellowships are for the academic year (September through May), though a few may be awarded for the fall or spring semester.

Applicant Eligibility: Applicants must hold a doctorate. Younger scholars should be engaged in work significantly beyond the revision of a doctoral dissertation. Scholars from any nation may apply for fellowships.

Application Requirements: Applicants must submit the center's application and financial forms (available on the Web site) supported by a curriculum vitae of no more than four pages, a 1,000-word project proposal, and three letters of recommendation.

Application Advice: One criterion in the selection process is that the project can be successfully pursued at the center. Be sure to read carefully the guidelines for the project description.

18. Woodrow Wilson Postdoctoral Fellowships in the Humanities

Administrative Agency: Woodrow Wilson National Fellowship Foundation

Address: Woodrow Wilson National Fellowship Foundation—Academic
   Postdocs
   CN 5281

Princeton, NJ 08543-5281
Phone: 609-452-7007; fax: 609-452-0066
Email: stevens@woodrow.org
Web: www.woodrow.org/academic_postdocs/

Deadline and Notification: November; finalists will be named via web site posting in December. At this time, the host institutions will conduct their own processes to decide to whom they will extend offers. Institutions make offers directly to selected candidates on or about February 1.

Number of Awards: 16 per competition.

Average Number of Applicants:

Other Related Fellowships: Mellon Postdoctoral Fellowships in the Humanities.

Award Amount: Minimum salary of $30,000 and benefits, office space, and research and library support.

Application Form: The application is on the web site.

Purpose of Grant/Fellowship and Restrictions: Sponsored in partnership with diverse U.S. colleges and universities (16 in 2001). The fellowship enables promising young teachers and scholars to "jump-start" careers during a difficult job market. It provides time and resources for research, dissertation prepublication revisions; broadens pedagogical experiences and abilities; encourages good practices in graduate education by emphasizing pedagogical experience, timely degree achievement, and meticulous scholarship.

Applicants may apply to up to five institutions with a single application. They may not apply to institutions where they did graduate work or were employed.

Length of Award: Two years.

Applicant Eligibility: Applicants must receive a Ph.D. in the humanities between December of the year before the deadline and June of the year after the deadline. They must hold a degree from accredited program in the United States or Canada that was earned in no more than seven years, including the M.A. work, unless there are exceptional circumstances. They must have significant teaching experience. Appointments will be made only if Ph.D. degree has been completed or dissertation filed. Open to U.S. citizens or permanent residents. Those holding other postdoctoral fellowships or tenure-track positions are not eligible.

Eligible fields of study are art history, classics, comparative literature, cultural anthropology, cultural studies (including all area studies), English literature, ethnic studies, foreign languages and literature, history, history and philosophy of science, history and philosophy of mathematics, interdisciplinary studies linguistics, music, history and theory, philosophy, political philosophy and theory, religion/religious studies, rhetoric, and women's studies.

Application Requirements: In addition to the application, a personal statement, summary of the dissertation, and c.v. must be sent via email attachment. Letters of recommendation may be sent as email attachments.

Index